BUSINESS RESPONSIBILITY IN ACTION

BUSINESS RESPONSIBILITY IN ACTION

Edited by

DAN H. FENN, JR.

Editor of the Harvard Business School Bulletin *and Member
of the Faculty of the Harvard Graduate School of Business Administration*

McGRAW-HILL BOOK COMPANY, INC.

New York Toronto London 1960

BUSINESS RESPONSIBILITY IN ACTION

20417

PREFACE

WHAT, EXACTLY, is "business responsibility?" A vague concept indeed, it seems to encompass a number of characteris-
tics which are supposed to distinguish the businessman of
today from his father and grandfather. It is a modern amal-
gam of corporate good citizenship, enlightened self-interest,
long-range planning, individual good citizenship, personal
ethics, and rational management.

According to the cliché of the moment, the business community today is different in kind, not just in degree, from
the men of the early 1900's. They were "robber barons" we
are told, living with no purpose other than profit, trampling
under lesser mortals in their stampede after the dollar. Their
belief in social Darwinism and their ready adoption of the

American flag and the Christian tradition as a cloak for their activities we scorn as hypocritical, even dangerous, nonsense.

No doubt it was, and perhaps these men would have left a happier memory for their descendants if they had been more honest with themselves. For this was an age which, apparently, demanded and condoned a single-minded pre-occupation with growth and expansion. We were willing to endure and forgive much in the interests of industrialization, and the voices of those who cried for a different set of values were drowned out by the roar of the steel mills and the clangor of the sledges in the hands of the railroad gangs. The important thing was to get on with the job.

If this is so, why do we now so sternly and self-righteously denounce these men? Why is it necessary for the business-man of today to disassociate himself so completely from his predecessors? They were doing their work in their time, just as we are doing ours in this.

Perhaps it is because the business manager is still unsure of the respectability of his chosen profession. Despite his success and influence, he may be troubled by the pocket of doubt about the nature of his contribution to society, a doubt which he cannot shake off. Possibly he is trying to convince himself and his neighbors that he is a fine fellow by com-paring himself with an ogre which he has set up as the image of the 19th century capitalist. If so, it is to his advantage to add yet a few more terrifying features to the creature to provide him with claws to go with his horns and tail to make him still more horrible by contrast.

This bogeymanism could be viewed as a mere historical oddity were it not that it is coloring the businessman's portrait of himself in 1960. By casting his forebears in the mold of a devil, he is casting himself in the mold of a god and making the same mistake his parents did. He wraps himself in all kinds of virtues—he says his objective is purely public service and his method of operations is good human relations guided by high if undefined ethical standards. So garbed, he places himself next to the synthetic 19th century monster he has helped to create.

But he is no god and his father was no devil. He is simply a human being, trying to do the best he can with the situation, ever balancing the short-range and the long, the "ought" and the "must," the democratic and the authoritarian. A manager and not an owner, more aware of the complex and lasting implications of his decisions, better trained and educated, more sensitive to the potential political power of the public, he is not as single-minded as those who walked these paths before him. His sense of responsibility is more a reflection of the changed circumstances than some remarkable transmutation in the species. He does not have all the answers any more than his father did, though he is certainly asking better questions.

Viewed in this framework, the thoughts and actions of businessmen described within this book do not stand as the final answers of the master group in our society. Rather they form a picture of some leaders trying to find their appropriate role in contemporary America. In so doing they provide some guidance and direction for the rest of us.

Warm appreciation is due the authors of this volume—the participants in the 29th Annual Conference of the Harvard Business School Association on which these pages are based. I owe special thanks, also, to Mrs. Alan Lebowitz for her skilled and experienced editorial hand which is evident throughout, and to Miss Elizabeth Knox for her preparation of the manuscript.

Dan H. Fenn, Jr.

CONTENTS

INTRODUCTION

Stanley F. Teele

THE PROGRAM COMMITTEE that planned the conference on
which this book is based set out to put together a series of
discussions and talks which would stir each member of the
audience to ask himself: How does this apply to me, to my
company, to my city; and what can I do about it?

As I listened to the oral presentations at the meeting, the
Twenty-ninth Annual National Business Conference held
by the Harvard Business School Association, I was impressed by the extent to which they had succeeded. Now,
having read this book which grew out of the sessions, I am
further struck by the exciting new areas which have been
opened up.

Note: Mr. Teele is Dean of the Harvard Business School.

For in these chapters we learn how men with imagination and vigor have thought through or implemented the bold new management concepts which were the highlights of the Harvard Business School Conference which marked our fiftieth anniversary in 1958.[1] The four areas selected—the company and the community, international operations, urban renewal, and business and politics—when coupled with the overview offered by Arthur Van Buskirk and Adlai E. Stevenson will, I hope, provide guidance and stimulation to the readers of this volume.

But the challenges of which they remind us are not new. As a matter of fact, we have been living with them through most of this century. Recently I was surprised to find that Brooks Adams, writing in 1913, was wrestling with the same basic issues with which we are concerned today. Nearly 50 years and two world wars ago, he prophetically pointed out that a modern society can hope to maintain a stable equilibrium in the midst of rapid change only by ensuring that it has among its administrators, both governmental and nongovernmental, a sufficient number who possess "a high order of generalizing mind—a mind which can grasp a multitude of complex relations." He added, significantly, that "this is a mind which can, at best, only be produced in small quantity and at high cost."

This warning has significance for all businessmen, and especially for those who have direct responsibility for the development of the younger managers who are just beginning their careers or working their way up through the

[1] See *Management's Mission in a New Society,* Dan H. Fenn, Jr., ed. (New York, McGraw-Hill Book Company, 1959).

echelons of the nation's companies. Perhaps the time has
come for business to put a heavier emphasis in their training
programs on the social and political context in which our
economic system functions. Up to now this material has been
considered strictly "blue sky" and has generally been pushed
aside for the specifics of marketing, accounting, and production. It may be that this attitude should be re-examined
in the light of the world in which we live and work.

Clearly, it is the responsibility of an institution like the
Harvard Business School to explore these areas, and we are
doing so. Our main task has always been to develop *com-
petence*—to help students acquire knowledge of the business
world and, from this foundation, to sharpen their skills for
decision making.

The background against which we undertake this job is
continually shifting. Big government has an impact on and
significance for the economy in ways that are now widely
accepted; from yesterday's vantage point, they would have
been viewed as hostile to a healthy business environment.
Corporate management has moved perceptibly from the old
concepts associated with ownership to a kind of stewardship
that recognizes a widening range of community and worker
interests. And management has suddenly discovered that it
may have to play a more dynamic role in politics if it is to
meet the challenge of opposing interests, ranging from labor
to government itself. But even though the background has
changed, I view our main task at the Harvard Business
School as still the same: helping young people acquire business knowledge and the ability to apply this knowledge
wisely to the solution of basic management problems.

Our second task has always been to develop attitudes appropriate to a business career. It is in this sphere, it seems to me, that we need to recognize the new urgency for an even greater degree of flexibility than we have had—one clearly commensurate with the new tempo and scope of change, both technical and social, which the contributors to this volume have so clearly sketched.

This school has always believed that the role of the manager calls for basic backgrounds reaching far beyond such fields as classical economics, accounting, and the theories of marketing. As we have seen the present challenge develop, we have attempted to stimulate fresh thinking about basic attitudes among both students and teachers.

In short, we are aiming to apply more effectively our familiar, tried-and-tested pragmatic approach to the solution of the maze of present-day issues by examining every new tool which shows any promise of helping to make decision making more of a science than the highly fallible art it still is. In so doing, we hope also that we are instilling in our graduates the habit of approaching their day-to-day problems with the same questioning attitude of the pragmatist who will always ask first and foremost: Is there really a problem and, if so, is this solution likely to work? I would like to suggest that those many men in both business and government who have taken this point of view have been the major architects of our present unique system—a system which we are increasingly recognizing as being different but as one which is generating productivity and power at a rate unprecedented in world history. I would further suggest that businessmen themselves may want to share this task with us.

YOUR COMPANY, ITS IMMEDIATE
FAMILY, AND ITS IN-LAWS

Editor's Note: This chapter is based on a panel discussion of the case of Linder Brothers, Inc. [1] The problem concerns the management's plan to relocate. It raises the resultant questions: for whom and to whom should the businessman be responsible in such an endeavor? Each member of the panel assumes a role in this situation. The participants are: Ken Bannon, Director of the Ford Department, United Automobile Workers—representing labor; Oliver T. Bergstrom, President of the Middlesex County National Bank in Boston—representing the potential lenders, the bank and the insurance company; Edmund W. Pugh, Jr., Vice President of the Columbia Broadcasting System—representing the stockholder group in favor of the move; Morris H. Wright, General Partner in Kuhn Loeb & Company—representing the stock-

[1] Disguised.

holders opposed to the move; General E. W. Rawlings, Financial Vice President of General Mills Corporation—representing the company's large customers. The moderator of the panel, George Albert Smith, Jr., is Professor of Business Administration at the Harvard Business School.

LINDER BROTHERS, INC.

Linder Brothers, Inc. manufactures dies and metal and plastic parts for sale to other manufacturers, including companies in the electronics industry. In recent years four large firms have accounted for 45% of Linder's total sales, which in 1958 were $2.33 million. The firm is located in downtown Boston, in a fairly old building and in a congested area with no room to expand. Equipment and production methods are not fully up to date, although the company is competitive and profitable. Because of the fast-moving nature of the industry, the company's top managers are somewhat apprehensive about the future, given their cramped quarters. They can do no more remodeling or readaptation.

The management recommended, early in 1959, that the company buy a plant site in Needham, Massachusetts, on Route 128, erect a building, and install some new machinery. The expectation was that with improvement of layouts and manufacturing processes, the current rate of output could be maintained with fewer workers, and an increase in capacity would be possible. From talks with customers, the managers feel that they could probably increase sales if they had more capacity. Furthermore, delivery and shipping would be simpler in a new, less congested location.

Seventy of the firm's 221 employees would be discharged. Those who continued would be obliged to travel considerably farther to and from work—a matter of 60 or 90 minutes more per day—and at greater expense.

The United Automobile Workers, representing 171 of the employees, has a contract with Linder Brothers under which any worker discharged because of plant movement or modernization receives one week's pay for each year of employment; the payments involved in the proposed move would cost the company an estimated $33,500. The local business agent of the union has not commented on the plan officially but has urged the company to stay in the present plant or retain all present employees in the new location.

To help finance the move, the company, which has a long tradition against borrowing, would negotiate a fifteen-month 5% bank loan for $427,000 and a fifteen-year 5½% mortgage loan for $960,000 from an insurance company. Also, the company would suspend for a year the annual $5 dividend paid on the 20,000 shares of outstanding stock. This proposal would increase its assets from $1.5 million to $2.6 million. In short, at the end of the move the company would be carrying a debt of $1.3 million, as against a net worth of $1.2 million in December 1958.

Some stockholders (no one person holds more than 15% of the stock) think the move is desirable; others think it is not, or at least they must still be persuaded. Boston city officials have urged the company not to move. Selectmen of Needham have urged the company to locate in their town. The company's large customers hope the move will be made.

Exhibit I. Summary data on proposed move of Linder Brothers, Inc.

Cash requirements for move:		
Plant and site	$1,132,500	
Less sale of old site	310,000	
Net cost of new plant		$ 822,500
Net cost of equipment		510,000
		$1,332,500
Moving costs		65,000
Contract settlement with employees		33,500
Estimating costs of moving (excluding interest)		$1,431,000
Interest costs (first year)		74,150
Total costs		$1,505,150
Cash sources to cover costs of moving:		
15-month 5% bank loan		$ 427,000
15-year 5½% mortgage loan		960,000
Total borrowing		$1,387,000
Cash on hand		118,150
Total cash		$1,505,150
Estimated annual labor saving:		
Direct labor (54 employees discharged)		$ 265,800
Indirect labor (16 employees discharged)		72,000
General employees (3 employees added)		(18,000)
Net labor saving		$ 319,800

Exhibit II. Profit and loss statements
(000 omitted)

	Year ending 12/31/58		Pro forma as of year ending 12/31/60 (Assuming move to Needham)	
Net sales	$2,330	100%	$2,330	100%
Less cost of goods sold:				
Materials	$820	35.2	$820	35.2
Direct labor	609	26.1	344	14.7
Indirect labor	324	13.9	252	10.8
State and local taxes ..	46	1.9	60 [a]	2.6
Depreciation	25	1.1	120	5.2
Other	69	3.0	64	2.7
	$1,893	81.2	$1,660	71.2
Gross profit	$ 437	18.8	$ 670	28.8
General and administrative expense	220	9.5	238	10.2
Earnings before interest	$ 217	9.3	$ 432	18.6
Interest charges:				
15-month loan (5%)			$ 21	
Mortgage loan (5½%)			53	
			74	3.2
Earnings before taxes	$ 217	9.3	$ 358	15.4
Federal income tax	108	4.6	179	7.7
Net profit	$ 109	4.7	$ 179	7.7
Less dividends	100			
To retained earnings	$ 9		$ 179	

[a] State and local taxes on a comparable plant in Boston proper would be $85,000.

Exhibit III. Balance sheets
(ooo omitted)

	As of 12/31/58	Pro forma as of 12/31/60 (Assuming move to Needham and repayment of bank loan)
Assets		
Cash	$ 235	$ 115
Accounts receivable	238	230
Inventory	546	545
Total current assets	$1,019	$ 890
Plant and equipment (net)	511	1,800
Total assets	$1,530	$2,690
Liabilities		
Accounts payable	$ 98	$ 100
Accruals	48	50
Tax liability	147	150
Total current liabilities	$ 293	$ 300
Loan (mortgage)		960
Capital stock	200	200
Retained earnings	1,037	1,230
Total net worth and liabilities	$1,530	$2,690
Net profit/Tangible net worth	8.8%	12.5%

EDMUND W. PUGH, JR.: As representative of a large group of stockholders, I think we should make the move and build this new plant. As long as we stay within our present four walls, we are limiting our future both physically and psychologically. We are not going to go out and try to get new business when we have limited productive capacity, and we may find it increasingly difficult to attract and hold our key management people. Furthermore, the sense of drive and the high morale of our organization may begin to suffer in time because of such a limitation on our future.

It is true that we are competitive today, but this might well prove to be only temporary. It is very dangerous for us to assume that our competitors will stand still or that no new factors will develop in the field. The American economy is moving ahead; it is growing. New techniques, new procedures, new processes are coming along every day, and this is especially true in our industry. If we don't put ourselves in a position to keep up, we will be done for.

I say, let's get on with this project.

MORRIS H. WRIGHT: The issue before us is not whether this company needs a new plant, or ought to build a plant. The progress of the company obviously depends upon it, so I don't want to debate that. The real issues are the risks in the timing and the extent of the proposal.

I am against this program because I believe the primary responsibility of management is not to any one of the groups involved—customers, stockholders, employees, or management—but rather to the enterprise itself. Self-preservation —the preservation of the firm—is the first principle involved here. This particular program is a threat to the very existence of the company. It involves taking on a terrific load of debt, actually in excess of the entire net worth.

Given the repayment schedule, and despite the willingness of a cautious New England banker to make the loan, it is an extremely hazardous venture. There are no margins for error; a strike, an interruption in the delivery of equipment or in the construction of the plant, will bring about the failure of the whole program.

OLIVER T. BERGSTROM: I might say that we at the bank stand for the same principles as does the dissenting stockholder group from which you have just heard. On the other hand, after careful study of this problem, we are convinced that Linder must do something. They cannot stand still; they must either fall behind or move ahead.

Specifically, we have confidence in the management group that has presented the case to us. They have demonstrated their ability to manage and manage properly. We agree with their evaluation of the situation, based on the figures they have shown us, the independent studies we have made, and an examination of the equipment presently employed in the manufacturing establishment. Furthermore, we must look at the industry itself. It is in a period of transition, becoming more highly automated all the time. Efficiency is becoming increasingly important in the competitive picture. While we agree that there is a substantial debt involved in this proposal, we do believe that there are some reserves for error—such as the potential improvement in volume and the added savings due to higher efficiency—so we look on this request as a little better than the average marginal loan, and we are willing to go along.

GENERAL E. W. RAWLINGS: I, too, am in favor of this move. It happens that three or four of us take about 45% or 50% of the output of Linder Brothers. We are involved in this new industry, the electronics field. I think you are all familiar with its expansion and development in the last few years, and the growth curve projected for the next few years.

At the same time, this is such a highly competitive industry that we have real problems of quality and delivery. We must have complete confidence in our supplier on both of these counts. Therefore, I can say flatly that the man who brings out the best quality product at the right price is going to get the business. If Linder does not—or cannot—keep up, we are in difficulty, and we will have to go elsewhere. We just cannot afford to take a chance.

I am concerned, too, about the matter of delivery. I would like to see Linder out on Route 128 since it would then be near our plant. Transportation costs would be cut for us, and rapid delivery assured. In addition, I might add, the move would give us an opportunity to work together on research and development programs, which are very important in this industry.

The only aspect of the move which worries me is the possibility of losing some or a majority of the labor force which has produced such a high-quality product at a good price in the past. But it seems to me the labor group has not recognized and understood the problems of the old plant. These people are working under very hazardous conditions, because of the dust in the factory, and I have some real questions about the health danger which apparently the union hasn't seen yet. And obviously all this dust and debris jeopardizes the quality of the new items being produced.

Given these facts, and looking ahead to the possibility of a substantial contract coming up, we are going to be forced to re-examine this matter of a supplier pretty soon. Personally, I would like very much to see this program put on the road.

KEN BANNON: I have discussed the contemplated move with the working force. We went into the problems that we have in this old building, such as the health hazard and the space limitations; we also recognize that expansion is beneficial for both the company and the workers.

However, we are opposed to the move that is being contemplated and the plan that was presented to us. We question the wisdom of it because the economics of the proposal are too risky. We agree, to a degree, with Mr. Wright in his evaluation.

We also are concerned, of course, about the fact that the work force is going to be substantially reduced. Further, those who would move with the jobs to Needham—the home town of the president of the company, by the way—will have to take on greater travel time and additional expense.

We think that Linder can step up its efficiency in the present facility and that expansion should take place gradually. We think the company should begin to bring new devices into its present plant; there hasn't been a new piece of equipment set up since 1946, and that, by the way, was a secondhand one. We have a four-product plant here, and expansion can take place product by product. We want to do this job gradually, starting with new machines and, possibly, a step-by-step move out of town. This kind of plan seems safer, more prudent, to us and easier on the work force as well.

RAWLINGS: I agree that this plan would have been possible several years ago, but management missed the boat. Speaking as a customer, we are very fortunate in having a young manager coming up who has vision and foresight, and can make the most out of this move. Furthermore, speaking very bluntly, I think that the possibilities of this business going into the ground are too great. This is a fast-changing industry. If Linder collapsed, the labor force would be out of jobs, an outcome which would obviously be far worse than having a few of them lose their positions now. Incidentally, I might say that we could conceivably work out an arrangement to take care of some of these men who would be let go.

BANNON: How are you going to "work that out"? I would be interested in knowing. Are you taking the responsibility for hiring any of these people who lose their jobs?

RAWLINGS: Obviously I couldn't do that. But there is a good possibility that many of the people will be able to get jobs in other spots because of the expanding nature of the industry in the whole area.

BANNON: That is a hope, but these men are going to be out of work on a definite day. They need more to live on than hope.

PUGH: We recognize that if we make this move, in order to protect the stockholders' interests, we are going to have to throw a good many people out of work. But it seems to me that business leadership has to face up to these conflicts and be courageous and clear-thinking about them. If the decision happens to result in 50 or 100 people being thrown out of work, that is just one of the facts of economic life in this country. We hope the unemployment will be temporary, and we certainly will try to get them relocated, but of course we can't guarantee success.

I think we all have to face the fact that these dislocations occur because of obsolescence; new and better ways of doing things are developed and have to be utilized. If management doesn't take advantage of them, it goes out of business in a highly competitive industry like this one. And you can't have these changes without somebody getting hurt, at least temporarily.

MODERATOR SMITH: But not all the stockholders believe that this move is in the stockholders' interests, do they Mr. Wright?

WRIGHT: This young president has been in office since 1939. He has taken advantage of the opportunities that every other company in this line of business has had; he got himself a good R & D staff, several government contracts with commercial possibilities, and a new product or two. He has demonstrated that he is an intelligent, far-sighted manager, and he has built up a good operation that is doing its job well in this boom-time.

But we don't know how much longer these good times and good breaks are going to last—certainly not forever. Are we going to mortgage the whole kit and kaboodle, chance it all on one throw of the dice? I believe in risk taking, but I'm not going to gamble my whole stake on one hand!

BERGSTROM: Gentlemen, I remind you that the previous speaker has consistently been a dissenting stockholder since 1939. He speaks very well, he is impressive, but the cold fact is that he is one of a group of people that has blocked a great deal of the progress this company might have made over the past several years.

I also remind you that this industry is not one which carries the less progressive elements along. Its entire development has taken place during the last five years. In the Needham and Cambridge area we are right in the middle of its fastest-moving segment. Every company in the field needs to increase its efficiency all of the time or suffer the consequences, dissenting stockholders to the contrary notwithstanding.

MODERATOR SMITH: I take it that you as a banker, Mr. Bergstrom, have responsibilities to your own stockholders and depositors and others. You are suggesting Linder Brothers is riding a new development, perhaps operating in a volatile industry, and yet you feel your bank should get into it?

BERGSTROM: I said that this was a new industry, not a volatile one. It has proved its staying power; it has proved its stability; it has proved its right to demand the attention of every well-operated financial institution.

WRIGHT: Methinks the banker doth protest too much!

MODERATOR SMITH: General Rawlings, are you on the edge of threatening this group? If they don't make this move might you take your business somewhere else?

RAWLINGS: Obviously one doesn't threaten his satisfactory supplier today, though I can't say that it has always worked that way in the past. In any event, what I was trying to point out is that in a highly competitive business like this one, we simply have to have a source of supply that turns out a high-quality product at a very favorable price. Looking forward, we are worried that Linder Brothers may be losing its competitive position. If you look at the figures over the years, the company is standing still, and standing still means going backwards.

MODERATOR SMITH: You talk with some enthusiasm about the possibility of expansion; you are not guaranteeing to take any more products from the company, are you?

RAWLINGS: No, we are going to go wherever we can get the best product at the best price.

MODERATOR SMITH: So the workers lose their jobs, and the company goes into debt on the strength of no stronger a commitment from you than that?

WRIGHT: I would like to ask General Rawlings one question. The program here calls for building a new plant, moving all the equipment, hiring such new workers as may be necessary, getting the organization all completed, and meeting their cash budget by making money again 90 days after the move. In your business experience, have you ever seen a company attain such a goal?

MODERATOR SMITH: You might say, even in New England?

RAWLINGS: Obviously this is a very tough program, and a difficult time schedule. But on the other hand, if the company doesn't approach it this way and attempt to meet that kind of schedule, it will never get there at all.

We have accomplished a great deal in this country with this kind of schedule. To be sure we have missed in many cases, but we have made progress by trying. Speaking for the customers, we think we are protected by the inventory we have on hand.

MODERATOR SMITH: Will you guarantee inventory?

RAWLINGS: Yes.

BANNON: Look, you people just aren't being realistic. Here you have a company with a net worth of $1.2 million, and no firm commitment as far as expansion is concerned. You are going out to the money market and borrow $1.3 million. The creditors are going to have more to say than the stockholders, really, after the loan is made. I don't think this is a healthy situation.

Then again you get into the matter of moving people from one plant to another, from one kind of machine to another. You don't transplant people like bushes, you know. You have a work force some of which has been employed since 1914 on one particular operation. Suddenly you are going to introduce them to this group of new machines, and they are going to ask, "What am I supposed to do with these?"

There is also a real question as to how many of the workers will go to the second location. Will you be able to have a trained work force at your second location? From the personnel standpoint alone, I don't think you can ever meet the commitment that General Rawlings talked about; from the viewpoint of the company's financial health, I think the proposal is suicidal.

The way to gain efficiency here is through a gradual expansion. For example, there are three screw machines in the plant. They are of 1908 vintage. If you were to introduce a new type of machine, you could do away with all three, and you would have one new piece of equipment producing more than the three are presently turning out. Furthermore, if the plant were expanded, or you built new facilities based on firm customer commitments, you could take the new piece of equipment and move it to the second location with your workers all trained.

WRIGHT: The issue isn't whether the company should have a new plant or modernize its equipment. Obviously that has to be done. The question is, how shall it be done and when should it be done? I think we should confine ourselves to some gradual program along the lines Mr. Bannon describes rather than putting the company in an impossible situation where it could be taken over by the creditors.

BERGSTROM: I would like to suggest again a careful examination of the figures which we have tried to pull together. The management has done a good job from an earnings standpoint over the last 20-year period. According to our figures, while the burden of repayment the first year is heavy, the plan should work. They will have cash available of $120,000 from depreciation and $30,000 from retained earnings, a total of $150,000 per year—a 10-year payout. They will make a labor saving of $320,000 a year. That should be more than adequate to retire the debt and to keep control of the company firmly in the hands of the directors and the stockholders. I see no formidable problem there.

As for the workers who presently live in the Chelsea-East Boston area, the trend is from the congested areas into the suburbs. Many of them are already moving into the Needham, Lexington, Concord area. So in a few years a Boston plant just won't be convenient for a large part of the work force.

MODERATOR SMITH: All those present want to see progress made, but at whose expense, and for whose gain? As Mr. Wright has pointed out, perhaps the question is not so much about whether this company should ever do anything, but what it should do, and when, and how it should be financed.

Mr. Bergstrom, would you be happier if Linder could manage this on a smaller loan? We are testing your margin, I take it.

BERGSTROM: Yes, if it could be done with a smaller loan, we would be pleased. But we are satisfied that this loan can be repaid and that it is in good proportion. Furthermore, we are impressed with the attitude of their accounts. While they are making no legal commitment to stay with Linder, the fact that they are here to plead the case is an indication of their desire to have this change made, and have it made now.

MODERATOR SMITH: Surely it is desirable from their viewpoint, but that doesn't change the fact that they are not agreeing to take the responsibility. They are not willing to underwrite the venture by contract or in any other way. I am not surprised that they are behind the move, and I don't think it means much. What have they got to lose?

BERGSTROM: Nevertheless, their presence is encouraging, certainly, to lenders in the picture.

PUGH: Mr. Moderator, you made a statement with which I cannot entirely agree. You said everybody here in this room is in favor of progress for this business. I am not sure that Mr. Bannon is really in favor of progress. I think that he is basically in favor of protecting the jobs of the workers.

BANNON: I started off by saying that we had talked this over, the work force and I, and we recognized that expansion was healthy. We also recognize that space is limited in the present facilities. I also stated that we think efficiencies can be accomplished by gradually undertaking some program like the one suggested. We also believe that the company can begin to build up cash reserves, something that hasn't been done since 1914 when the company first was born, if this proposal is carried out piecemeal instead of in one bite.

We are strictly opposed to shutting this plant down today and setting a new one up tomorrow. Make no mistake about that. Furthermore, we question the figures that you have given to us with respect to the potential manpower reduction. We think you will find yourselves very much on the low side as far as your indirect labor is concerned when you begin to automate the new facilities.

So far as the present facility is concerned, we would like to take this molding job, which is the health hazard we have talked about, and put it in a second location, making it a unit by itself. After you have the second location in operation, surely you are not going to move the existing screw machines in there and again create a health hazard. Rather, as the market for the molding process expands, you would take the new-type screw and die machinery and move it into the new facilities. Thus, you go through the costly moving and purchase process a step at a time as the market grows to handle it.

During this period of time you would not be hiring new personnel, and those who would have been laid off as a result of the move would not lose seniority or job rights. You would have trained manpower at your fingertips. As operations at the new location prospered, you people of course would be able to call these laid-off people back to work.

In other words, the basic objective you have in mind is fine, but the way you are going about it, in our opinion, involves too big a gamble. We have a stake in this, too; if the company goes bankrupt, we have a contract but no jobs, and we can't eat a contract.

PUGH: Mr. Bannon, you talk about the possibility of two locations. The gross margin in this business now is about

18%. You are recommending two separate locations, which is bound to increase administrative costs and general overhead. Although we can't work the figures out here, that would produce a reduction in the gross margin which is already pretty tight and subject to great hazards competitively.

MODERATOR SMITH: You believe no company should operate at two locations?

PUGH: Here we have a small company, as companies go.

MODERATOR SMITH: You want it to grow. You said growth is the whole secret—grow or die.

PUGH: That is right. If we ever get big enough, two or more locations may be all right. At this size, where we have a limited force, you can't help but compound your problems if you operate at both locations.

MODERATOR SMITH: Are you arguing against moving piecemeal?

RAWLINGS: It could be done economically.

BANNON: As we mentioned, the net worth of the company was $1.2 million from 1947 up to the present time. The stockholders received $100,000 each year in dividends over a period of twelve years, or $1.2 million—a sum equal to the net worth of the company over a 12-year period. If you were to adopt our approach, the stockholders wouldn't get quite as much. You would be putting it into the new facilities and equipment.

MODERATOR SMITH: Let me take another tack. Some of you are implying that the company would be more profitable if it did move. Correct?

PUGH: Either more profitable, or, if competitors did the same thing virtually simultaneously, it would at least protect its profit position.

MODERATOR SMITH: I wonder if you and General Rawlings are gambling on two opposite possibilities, then. You, Mr. Pugh, are rather hoping it would be more profitable, or at least as profitable, while the General is hoping that his costs as a purchaser will go down a little bit.

PUGH: It is only natural that the General and I should have somewhat opposite hopes, for he is a purchaser and I am a stockholder. I think there is an inevitable conflict of interest built in here. But I would hope that once we get into the new plant with its greater productive capacity, our sales force will become more aggressive; if they can't sell the General more business, I expect them to find other customers who will provide us with an over-all increase in our business.

MODERATOR SMITH: Perhaps here is an alternative to a move now. Why not get this extra business, if it is indeed available, and do some subcontracting with it at the moment. In other words, be sure you have the business, hang on to your workers at the present plant, and then make the shift. Make certain that General Rawlings and his friends will come through!

PUGH: In this business, the basic profit is on the manufacturing. If you subcontract it out, you give away to the subcontractor a great deal of the profit, and what you then realize is as an effective jobber, not as a manufacturer. Profit-wise, I don't think this would be too attractive a return on investment.

MODERATOR SMITH: It may be better than giving the company away to the bank.

WRIGHT: I wonder if I could point out one or two facts? The normal earnings of the company average a little over $100,000 a year, although there was a period of about 10 years when there were no earnings.

BERGSTROM: Not since the present management took over, however.

WRIGHT: That is right. Now the amount of projected increase on these estimates, $50,000 a year, is an increase in earnings of approximately 50%. To realize that money we have to put in as much as we have invested in the business now. From the standpoint of additional return, it certainly is not as attractive to get the additional earnings as it is to keep what we are now getting on our present capital.

The one area where there is no conflict of interests is in the preservation of the enterprise. I can't believe that it is prudent for the company to undertake an indebtedness of about $1.4 million on top of another $300,000 in the current budget, or $1.7 million, with a normal earning power of a little over $100,000 a year. Thirteen years of earnings are being put on the line here. Any estimates of future improvement are just that—estimates!

MODERATOR SMITH: Mr. Bergstrom, you are a banker in the area; does this management have any responsibility to the city of Boston, which has provided services for the company and its workers for years?

BERGSTROM: I am sure it does, and I think management has recognized this relationship for a long time. It has tried to work with the city in order to ease the transition. It recognizes that the central city is vital to its continued growth, no matter where in the area the actual plant may be located.

On the other hand, I think management takes the viewpoint that its first obligation is to itself. By moving into a location that will be more efficient in operation, with more pleasant surroundings and room for expansion, it is following the laws of economics. It will do everything possible to be a help to the city—selling its existing plant, and so on—but basically the city must solve its own problems.

SUMMARY[2]

Our purpose in using a discussion of an actual problem was to dramatize or, if you will, to emphasize the conflicts of interest which arise when a rather typical, but consequential, business decision is being made. In the mind of the conscientious manager faced with such a tangle of points of view, the question must inevitably frame itself: To whom and for whom am I responsible, and in what amounts?

It is very easy for us to agree on generalizations, especially in this area of business responsibility. The glib phrases roll

[2] By the moderator, George Albert Smith, Jr.

out of the mouths of service-club speakers as easily as they do from the typewriters of journalists or the pens of professors. "The thing to do," we say, "is be fair, make the reasonable decision, be a responsible citizen." But when we leave the inspirational luncheon speaker behind and start to wrangle with an actual problem on our desks, it does not look so simple any more. "Just what is 'fair'?" we ask ourselves, "and what is 'reasonable' and 'responsible'?"

In the discussion which you have just read, it was clear that everyone spoke with good will and with the firm desire to see Linder Brothers survive and grow. No one was trying to torpedo the company or its management. The knotty issue was how the growth could best be accomplished; the conflicts boiled up out of different personalities, backgrounds, and, perhaps most important, differing frames of reference. If representatives of the city of Boston and the town of Needham had been present, this type of confrontation might have been even more clear.

Furthermore, no one wants unnecessarily to hurt anyone else. There are no personal feuds or vendettas in evidence here. At the same time, everyone apparently recognizes that the proposed change does inevitably involve benefits to some and losses to others. I take it that the challenge to a business manager is to be as sure as he can that if someone gets hurt the reason is sufficient and that the over-all gain for society offsets the damage done. Making this kind of judgment imposes a heavy burden on a businessman, and to make it honestly demands a high degree of intellectual honesty, objectivity, humility, and wisdom.

What is the president of Linder Brothers to do? To whom and for whom is he responsible? One answer, of course, is "to his stockholders. They own the company; their money sustains it." But how much help is this reply? In the first place, the stockholders are not unanimous. Does the company management owe nothing to the minority point of view?

Secondly, are the stockholders really in a position to know where their best interests lie? Isn't it possible that a move which was opposed to the interests of the workers as they conceived those interests would be so damaging that the owners would suffer in the long run?

How about the city of Boston? In a later chapter in this book there is a discussion of the responsibility of a business toward the community which provides it shelter. Boston is trying to navigate a narrow and shoal-filled channel; it is fighting a battle against rot and stagnation. Without Boston, there would be no metropolitan area; without a metropolitan area, there would be no Linder Brothers. Can this obligation, either from a moral or a practical standpoint, be dismissed quite as casually as Mr. Bergstrom indicates?

What about customers? There seems to be little evidence that General Rawlings either can be or wants to be especially responsible to Linder. He wants them to move; he even threatens a little, but he offers no guarantees. Does a company feel under any obligation to its customers under these circumstances? In a fast-moving industry like electronics, if it does not feel under such an obligation, regardless of how the customer views the situation, how long will it survive?

Perhaps the basic responsibility is the one Mr. Wright keeps stressing: to the company itself and its survival. Maybe self-preservation is the final arbiter; but neither this country nor this industry was built solely on that philosophy. Instead, businessmen—and the rest of us, too—have felt responsible to a set of ideals: "progress," "enterprise," "growth," "better products and wider distribution," and the like. To what degree is the business manager in America today, especially considering Governor Stevenson's remarks in his chapter, responsible to concepts like these?

Then there is Mr. Bannon's work force: highly skilled, loyal people. Are they, in Bannon's words, to be "transplanted like bushes?" Can you—should you—treat them in the apparently casual manner displayed by General Rawlings and Mr. Pugh, who expressed "hope" and "confidence" that the workers would all find good jobs quickly enough?

It is at this point that another dimension comes in: To whom and for whom does the general public consider a company responsible? With an increased willingness to use government to accomplish its ends in the economic field, and with various other devices at its disposal, the community reputation held by a company is important. So Linder's president has to consider not only where he thinks his responsibilities lie but also how the community sees those responsibilities.

As you read the discussion and ponder the situation, you will be able to discover still other areas of obligation—the government, the national interest and the need to accelerate our economic growth, the industry, the R & D people who need pleasant surroundings and adequate facilities. How a man steers his way through this series of reefs depends, in the last analysis, on two factors: the particular situation, including the timing, and his own set of values. The decision he makes on one occasion may not be appropriate the next time; suppose that the discussion we have read took place in war time, for instance. As for his own scale of standards, this is built up of what he thinks is really important. For Linder himself, it might be security; it might be growth; it might be a unified group of stockholders; it might even be having the plant located near his own home!

My hope, and that of the members of the panel, is that this chapter will be able to stimulate the reader to steer clear of substituting glib generalizations in this area of business responsibility for hard thinking; and that it may raise the question of whether the ultimate responsibility may not be to the process of picking up, examining, assessing, and weighing each of the conflicting interests that are bound to develop in any business situation.

YOUR COMPANY AND YOUR COMMUNITY: THE LESSONS OF PITTSBURGH

Edward C. Bursk

WHAT RESPONSIBILITY does the businessman have to his own community? What particular talents can he contribute? What changes in his customary approach or attitude will he need to make if he is to be effective? What kinds of potholes and roadblocks can he expect to encounter if he tries to accomplish something worthwhile?

To throw some light on these questions, this chapter deals with one of the outstanding examples of business leadership

Note: This chapter was based on a panel discussion and prepared by Edward C. Bursk, Professor of Business Administration at the Harto come out of postwar America: the Pittsburgh Renaissance. In this still-continuing story, a group of businessmen combined forces with the political leaders to work great changes in what was once a desperate city.

There are two parts to the Pittsburgh story. One is the dramatic list of accomplishments; but this has been widely publicized. The other, hidden beneath the surface and much more relevant to our purposes, is the series of conflicts and triumphs and frustrations out of which the renaissance was built. It is from this part of the story that businessmen elsewhere can learn the lessons of Pittsburgh.

In a recent speech, Arthur Van Buskirk [1] described the beginning of the rebuilding of Pittsburgh:

> Our city came out of the war with a bleak outlook. It was smoky and unattractive. There was a woeful lack of recreational opportunities; the housing was poor. No major expressway had been built and none was in design. Urban blight was making deep and telling inroads throughout the city—especially in the Golden Triangle. Local steel leaders

vard Business School and Editor of the *Harvard Business Review,* who served as moderator. The panel participants were: Jervis J. Babb, Chairman of the Area Development Committee of the Committee on Economic Development; John J. Grove, Assistant Director of the Allegheny Conference on Community Development; David L. Lawrence, Governor of Pennsylvania; John T. Ryan, Jr., President of the Mine Safety Appliances Company and President of the Allegheny Conference; and William P. Snyder, III, President of the Shenango Furnace Company and recently retired Chairman of the Allegheny Conference.

[1] Mr. Van Buskirk is one of the contributors to this volume. See p. 125.

were pessimistic about Pittsburgh's future steel prospects. Many of the corporations that had long made their headquarters in Pittsburgh were considering plans to move out. There was no civic pride and many of the younger people were planning to settle elsewhere, as they considered postwar careers.

And then an amazing thing happened—an event that occurs only once in generations of a community's history. A whole group of younger men and new leaders came into positions of executive responsibility in Pittsburgh's industrial life. With new vision and greater social consciousness sharpened by experiences in World War II, this group under the leadership of Richard K. Mellon decided to marshal the full energies and resources of the community behind a united effort to tackle the city's problems and carry forward a bold and imaginative improvement program.[2]

According to the folklore of the city, this enterprise was actually sparked when General Richard Mellon, back in town after several years' absence during World War II, awoke in his hotel room the first morning and looked out the window. He was appalled by what he saw: a city that was so smoky the lights had to be left burning at midday. "I had forgotten how bad this is," he is reported to have said. "Something is going to have to be done."

So he enlisted Van Buskirk in the effort, and the Allegheny Conference on Community Development was formed. This group, made up primarily of business leaders, was de-

[2] "What Business Has Learned About Rebuilding a City," Committee for Economic Development meeting, May 29, 1958.

signed to supply the muscle to implement the ideas and technical know-how which already had been developed over some years by the Pittsburgh Regional Planning Association. Without the power plant represented by the Conference, the possibilities in Pittsburgh remained simply sketches on a shelf, ideas in a planner's mind.

Happily for Pittsburgh, David Lawrence was Mayor of the city as this effort got under way. His effective political leadership, harnessed with the business influence as represented by the Conference, made possible the implementation of the plan for a new city.

The first problem was smoke control; here was a health menace, a piece of bad public relations, and a real drag on the morale of the whole community. Charles Dickens, way back in 1840, is supposed to have called Pittsburgh: "hell with the lid off"; certainly by 1940 it was notorious throughout America for its Stygian gloom. If only this one could be beaten, the Conference would be off to a good start and, so the theory went, the city would be more willing to support other ventures.

At this point, one of the real lessons of Pittsburgh emerged; no matter how good the project and how powerful the forces trying to push it, there will always be sturdy, resourceful, vigorous opposition. In this instance, some business concerns fought the proposed smoke ordinances because of the heavy expenses involved; some homeowners did battle because they would be forced to change their heating systems from soft to hard coal or other types of smokeless fuels; some politicians, notably one city councilman, rose up out of a sincere dislike of the scheme or a smell of a political issue— or a combination of the two.

The passage and enforcement of the smoke ordinances proved to be a long, drawn-out, see-saw proposition which is still continuing. It turned out to be a county-wide issue instead of just a city one. It became involved in municipal management and business sensitivities with questions over the location of the inspection and enforcement processes. Finally, the leaders of the Allegheny Conference discovered, it is a chore which has to be worked at on a regular, continuing basis. The job is never tied up and done with.

Out of these years of uphill work has come a dramatically successful program. As the accompanying illustrations show, smoke has been cut between 85% and 90% and Pittsburgh got a new lease on life. Its morale received a boost, and there were some tangible results from the Conference and its labors.

The smoke control story has been duplicated in instance after instance. New highways and bridges, the clearing and redevelopment of the Golden Triangle and Point Park, the slum removal in the Lower Hill, the construction of the municipal auditorium—all meant tireless efforts to overcome opposition. Legal battles up to and including the Supreme Court of the United States, political and business pressures, complaints from householders and small businessmen in areas marked for redevelopment, concern with historical sites like the old cemetery that stood in the projected path of the new thruway—all these and many more dominate the history of this huge endeavor. It took determination and power—both business and political—to carry through these and other projects.

This chapter is based on a discussion of the Pittsburgh experience by four men who actually participated in the program, augmented by one man with a national perspective. From this interchange, four particularly significant questions arose which are pertinent for business managers who are concerned with this area of community responsibility. They were:

(1) How do you line up and maintain business support for this kind of venture?

(2) How can cooperative relations be worked out with political leaders?

(3) What order of priorities for projects should be established?

(4) What is the businessman's stake in the refurbishing and rejuvenating of our cities?

Let us look at each of these topics in turn and see what the panel had to say about it. Out of their exploration of these issues, others may catch flashes which will illuminate some of the realities of community responsibility.

Lining Up Business Support

In Pittsburgh, under the leadership of Richard Mellon, and other top businessmen, the Allegheny Conference has

Downtown Pittsburgh before smoke control—1945. (Photo by Allegheny Conference on Community Development.)

Same view of downtown Pittsburgh after smoke control—1955. (Photo by John R. Shrader, Swager Studio.)

Scene in downtown Pittsburgh with smoke blanketing the Triangle—prior to smoke control. (Photo by Newman-Schmidt Studios.) Below, Mellon Square in the midtown Triangle. (Photo by Samuel A. Musgrove.)

Top, Pittsburgh's Golden Triangle in 1950—prior to any redevelopment. (Photo by John R. Shrader, Swager Studio.) Middle, Pittsburgh's Golden Triangle—Fall of 1959. (Photo by Samuel A. Musgrove.) Bottom, The Triangle as it will appear tomorrow. (Photo by Newman-Schmidt Studios.)

The Lower Hill adjoining the Golden Triangle—prior to clearance.
(Photo by Department of City Planning.)

Architect's sketch of the new public auditorium under way in the Lower
Hill. (Photo by John R. Shrader, Swager Studio.)

had real success in developing major support. Governor Lawrence starts off the discussion of this topic:

GOVERNOR DAVID L. LAWRENCE: I want to say this for the business interests of Pittsburgh: I never asked one man to serve on an authority, a commission, or a committee of any sort who refused to do so. That record is a measure of the spirit of the business leaders; they really wanted to put the projects over.

MODERATOR BURSK: That sounds unbelievable. It seems impossible that every businessman could have this spirit, but I suppose once something like this gets going it is easier.

Wasn't it hard to rally the businessmen at the start at least? Maybe they were willing to accept official city posts later, but how about the Allegheny Conference?

WILLIAM P. SNYDER, III: We have an Executive Committee in the Allegheny Conference which numbers seventeen. We take our turn serving on that, and here again nobody has ever refused when asked to serve, no matter how high his business position.

JOHN J. GROVE: We have more than 500 business leaders participating on various authorities, commissions, and committees that have been set up in the city and county to carry out this program. They are people like Fred Foy, President of the Koppers Company, who is President of the Pittsburgh Civic Business Council, one of our civic agencies. George G. Main, Vice President in Charge of Finance of the Westinghouse Electric Corporation, is the Chairman of the Public Parking Authority. Edmund S. Ruffin, Jr., Vice President and General Counsel, Koppers Company, is Chairman of the Allegheny County Sanitary Authority. Henry L. Hillman, President of the Pittsburgh Coke and Chemical Company, is a member of the Pittsburgh Urban Redevelopment Authority. So the list goes.

JOHN T. RYAN, JR.: The county commissioners have appointed an advisory committee for the new, huge county hospital for the aged sick which represents an investment of $22 million. Carl A. Brinkman, Treasurer of H. J. Heinz Corporation, is on the committee, as are a number of other corporate executives. To cite just one more example, Clifford F. Hood, President of United States Steel until his recent retirement, is Chairman of the Airport Advisory Committee for the Greater Pittsburgh Airport, another county facility.

'GROVE: Needless to say, all these business leaders serve without pay on these commissions, and in many instances they devote every bit as much time to the agencies as they do to their own private businesses.

SNYDER: The business people in Pittsburgh have now really developed the habit of participating and working in the various renaissance projects.

MODERATOR BURSK: All right, but how do you get to this point?

RYAN: One important fact is that we do not accept anybody by proxy in the Conference. In other words, if we ask the president of the company, we want the president. We don't want the fifth vice president in charge of extracur-

ricular activities. This gives the whole enterprise status
and prestige.

SNYDER: That policy certainly was vital, and paid off especially when we had to get company backing for specific
projects. In carrying out the Gateway Center business development financed by Equitable Life, for example, we had
to persuade nine Pittsburgh corporations to sign a twenty-
year lease with Equitable Life before the ground could be
broken. Only the top man in the corporation can make that
decision. But of course we do not select a man just because he
is the head of a big corporation. It is a combination of his
personality plus what he represents. We are not interested in
a lot of big names for the sake of window-dressing.

MODERATOR BURSK: You pick him for his ability and his
willingess to give up a lot of time?

SNYDER: Time is not the factor it was a few years ago, when
we were starting. The program does not require the time it
did in the beginning.

MODERATOR BURSK: You would say, wouldn't you, that
Pittsburgh was desperate in 1947? I am not trying to take
any credit away from what was accomplished, but it is true
that you had a crisis on your hands and an unusually powerful business leader—Richard Mellon—who was determined
to do something about it. And you had a strong, enlightened
political leader in David Lawrence. Isn't this happy combination of circumstances the real answer to your success in lin-
ing up business support?

SNYDER: I certainly think we were helped by this coincidence of events. They got us started. But we all sincerely feel that other cities, if they approach it with a will, can do the same thing.

JERVIS S. BABB: I might point out, too, that plenty of other cities are in as desperate a plight as Pittsburgh was in 1947. It's just that they have not fully realized it yet.

LAWRENCE: Richard Mellon, granted the importance of his leadership, would be the last person in Pittsburgh to allow an impression to get abroad that he is the fellow who did it. The same is true of me in my part of the job. One or two people cannot do something like this alone. Without literally thousands of participants at various levels, from enthusiastic support to actual working responsibilities, a face-lifting like this cannot be carried through.

BABB: Somebody has to start. Somebody has to be the person to set people to work in this area. Every community has one or two top men to start off on this road, if they are really concerned. The initiators may not be Mellons or Lawrences, but in their own areas they carry tremendous influence if they once start to use it.

MODERATOR BURSK: In other words, you are saying that Pittsburgh may have been unique in the depth of the crisis and the magnitude of the power of men like Mellon and Lawrence, but that basically the same situation exists elsewhere if people really get steamed up over the need for action.

BABB: That is so, and there are plenty of examples: Philadelphia, Baltimore, Chicago, South Bend, New Haven.

MODERATOR BURSK: How about the situation today? I understand you have stirred up opposition; the job you have done was too bold not to step on some toes. Has this opposition been building up as you go along?

GROVE: We had opposition to smoke control from special interests. Now we are fighting for mass transportation legislation, and some local interests are opposed to it. As a matter of fact, we have had to fight every inch of the way against minority blocs, often with perfectly legitimate grounds for disagreeing with us when viewed from the standpoint of their own immediate situation. But we have not yet reached the point where these have consolidated into a majority of opposition to the entire enterprise, and we think that they will not do so as long as we are doing a good job.

MODERATOR BURSK: But can you keep your support at such a peak? The Allegheny Conference itself used to be financed by a general drive that included other agencies; now it must turn to the business community on its own behalf. The big, dramatic projects are behind you, to some extent: will businessmen back such drab, though vital, developments like mass transportation, sewage disposal, and housing? Up to now, the program has had little impact on the tax rate since it has been financed by federal and private funds; when the businessman's bill goes up, will he still be in your corner?

GROVE: As you indicate, the situation is changing, and we cannot be certain what this new phase will mean to us. But we have met tough challenges in the past; we are aware of the possibility that our problems tomorrow will be slightly

different; and we are working on plans which we hope will
equip us to surmount them.

Cooperation with City Hall

Without a close, informed relationship between the businessmen and the politicians, it will be highly difficult for a
city to move off dead center. The fact of the matter is that
the constraints that are binding our great urban centers can
only be cut by a combination of political action and private
financial initiative. Zoning ordinances, public transportation,
action against smog, recreational areas, traffic, and a host of
other topics come under the purview of municipal government. Without its power of eminent domain and its rights
and financial tools under urban renewal programs, a project
like Pittsburgh's is stymied. On the other hand, without private developers and private financing, powerful public support, business confidence, and management skills, no effort
will get very far.

The original impetus may come from either the public or
the private sector, but unless both are enthusiastically and
effectively committed, the venture is likely to flounder.

But businessmen are unused to dealing with politicians—
at least, on the basis of mutual support and confidence—and
friction can develop quickly. Here is what the Pittsburghers
had to say on this issue.

BABB: I think Pittsburgh was very fortunate in having a
mayor who understood the businessman. Happily, too, it had

businessmen who believed that a man elected to political office might be a good citizen economically, and understand business problems as well as social ones. As a result of the cooperation of City Hall and the business community, a great job has been done in Pittsburgh.

Now I suspect there are many businessmen who do not have the same understanding of and confidence in the politician, or live in communities where the mayor does not seem to have respect for the businessman. Do you have any suggestions as to how these people can get together—because oftentimes the stickiness comes primarily from a lack of contact and from ill-based suspicion?

LAWRENCE: Of course this kind of cooperation has not been common in our cities for many years, and the lack of it has held our urban areas back. We must admit that it is a little difficult to accomplish, and that there are some built-in obstacles.

For example, in my city, the city administration is Democratic; the city government is Democratic; the county government is Democratic. A great deal of the state administration was Republican, and the national administration was Democratic, when we started; then it turned around and became Republican, and the state administration switched to Democratic. To the politician, the welfare of his party is vitally important both professionally and emotionally, and it is not easy for him to rise above this partisanship and accomplish ends that may help the other side.

Likewise the businessmen have to make some adjustments.

In Pittsburgh, and in many other cities, all the real wealth is among Republicans. These businessmen are the big contributors to Republican campaign funds. Yet the city governments with which they must work are primarily Democratic.

Speaking for the politician, it is important to gain the confidence of the business community. A Democratic mayor has to show that his primary purpose in undertaking a project like this one is not to make political capital, but to do something that needs to be done for the city. I remember an incident when we started on the program for redevelopment. In telling this story I may sound a little vain, but it is useful nevertheless because it gets across the spirit that was abroad at the time.

I had in mind setting up the Redevelopment Authority with Arthur Van Buskirk as the chairman. So after we passed the ordinance establishing the Authority, I said to him, "I want you to be its first chairman." His reply surprised me. "No," he said, "we have decided you ought to be chairman." "But that is ridiculous," I answered. "Under the ordinance, the mayor has to appoint the Authority. It would be foolish for me to appoint myself. The people will laugh at me."

Mr. Van Buskirk understood my point, so he went out and got the newspapers to publish editorials asking me to take the chairmanship. I agreed to do so, but in appointing the Authority I made what I feel was a wise decision. I appointed three Republicans and two Democrats. This one move, I believe, did more to convince the businessmen of

Pittsburgh that we were sincerely nonpartisan in this effort than any other single action we took. It earned us the confidence of the people in general, and of Republican business in particular, and set the tone for the whole project. As a result, we never discuss partisan politics where Pittsburgh is concerned.

MODERATOR BURSK: Was this a matter of strategy on your part?

LAWRENCE: Yes. I figured that this was one way I could give evidence of good faith, and I needed plenty among the Republicans because I had not only been the Democratic mayor, but the political leader of Pittsburgh as well. To the opposition, I was known as the boss, in the old-time political sense, and I had to live that down.

SNYDER: I would like to say about my good friend "Mayor Paul Bunyan" here, that we probably have all disagreed with him politically. The members of the Conference are for the most part Republicans. But we have seen this cooperative relationship flourish, and we know it exists even though we admit that it is very difficult to explain to others.

RYAN: Speaking as a businessman, one of the great benefits I have gained from my experience in this project is my association with Governor Lawrence. I have learned that the businessman has to appreciate the problems of the man in political life. He has to acquire a sense of the political realities, which are somewhat apart from his way of life and the approach he takes to his own problems. The politician, as a professional, has to get elected, just as a business manager has

to make a profit if he is to accomplish anything. Furthermore, the businessman is used to dealing with problems in
his own business and industry, where he can simply say,
"We are going to do this job this way," and he can pretty well
expect it to be done. But the politician has to deal with conflicting views, with a host of public relations questions far
more complex and immediate than ours.

LAWRENCE: Both sides display a certain amount of timidity
in making the first contact. The average businessman and
the average public official are a little afraid of each other,
because they come from different worlds. That gap has to
be bridged, and it *can* be with patience, open-mindedness,
and a willingness to learn.

MODERATOR BURSK: But you do not claim to be an average
politician, do you?

LAWRENCE: Yes. I like to get re-elected as much as the next
man in my business.

GROVE: It is true, nationally and at the community level,
that there are always men of little faith. There are politicians
who are suspicious that the businessman is *only* interested in
making money, just as there are business managers who hold
the mistaken notion that the one and only goal of the man in
politics is to get re-elected—at any cost. When Governor
Lawrence, as the Mayor of Pittsburgh, appointed the Redevelopment Authority, it included representatives of United
States Steel which held vast properties in the upper part of
the Triangle. Because this area is a mile away from the site
of the then projected Gateway Center development, many

people said, "That board is not going to do anything serious about this project because it is against their best economic interests. It will decrease their property values by making the renewed area much more desirable than the old." Nevertheless they did, and today both sections have gained and profited enormously. In fact they are booming.

MODERATOR BURSK: Isn't this fact the real key to the success of your joint enterprise? There is no secret, no mystery, about the reason for the closeness of your business-political cooperation: it is simply that this relationship works out, in the long run, in the best interests of both sides.

BABB: Yes, certainly business in Pittsburgh and in other cities where redevelopment programs are under way has benefited substantially from an economic standpoint.

LAWRENCE: I think this mutual self-interest and mutual belief in the whole community is precisely the answer. As the mayor of another city which is rebuilding itself once said, "What's good for the city is good for City Hall."

For my part, I believe that being a good mayor is the best way to stay in office, and my own political record seems to bear this out. The first time I was elected by 14,000; then I entered into the spirit of the movement with the Allegheny Conference. I ran the next time and won by 56,000, the next time by 55,000, and the last time by 60,000. And in my campaign for Governor I carried the city by 70,000. This shows that the people appreciate it when you do a job, and that it does not hurt you at the polls when you cooperate with the business interests.

GROVE: I might add that Governor Lawrence was the first third-term mayor in Pittsburgh history, and then went on to be elected to a fourth term.

Setting Priorities

What needs to be done in a city? The answer to this question depends, of course, on the community, but Pittsburgh's dilemma was not so unique as to be of no value to the rest of us.

GROVE: We began in the Golden Triangle, in the central business district, because it is the economic heart of the Pittsburgh region. We felt that unless the heart was healthy, we could not hope in any way to create a general well-being throughout the region. We are now moving out into other areas in the cities and counties.

MODERATOR BURSK: The problem was an economic one to begin with, and this is the way you tackled it?

GROVE: Yes. We felt that unless the city was strong economically we could not carry out a broad-scale community program.

MODERATOR BURSK: But what about the problems of suburbia? Can you actually tackle the central city without dealing with the environs too?

GROVE: In every city, as Arthur Van Buskirk says in his chapter, there is a great population explosion. Most of these new families are settling in the suburban areas, and this fact certainly has a heavy impact on the core of the area—the city itself. Our situation in Allegheny County is like that of most other metropolitan areas. We have 129 municipalities in Allegheny, and Pittsburgh happens to be the largest. But the 1950 census shows that more people in Allegheny County now live outside the corporate limits of the city than within Pittsburgh itself. This is a serious problem for the future, and by saying that we started in town I do not mean that we have stopped there.

RYAN: After all, the name of the Conference is the *Allegheny* Conference, not the Pittsburgh Conference. Some of us are now coming to feel even this is not big enough; that we need an outlook broader than even that of a county.

MODERATOR BURSK: When you start thinking this way, you run into a mesh of entrenched ideas and local pride, don't you? You uncover a host of concepts which are fine in their own way but which would stand in the path of the development of the total community.

LAWRENCE: You are absolutely right, and this is another reason for moving in on the city first. In our case, the word "metropolitan" is anathema to most people. The little communities and the little political leaders—and it applies equally to both parties—do not want to give up their domains. Because they refuse to be absorbed into the city, we cannot do as many things as we would like.

To some extent, we have met the problem by transferring many of the activities of the city to the county government, which is strong in Pennsylvania. The Health Department is county-wide in Allegheny County, as is the Welfare Department; and we are now tackling the transit problem on a county basis.

MODERATOR BURSK: Most of the projects you have talked about have been economic. They have been primarily physical changes like clearing away slums, putting up buildings, and so on. Recently, Leland Hazard, who is now a Professor at Carnegie Tech but was General Counsel of Pittsburgh Plate Glass and a participant in your project, raised questions along these lines. Here are some excerpts from a speech he made:

> We have not yet admitted that the real size of our metropolitan community is much greater than existing political boundaries would indicate....
>
> We are slow to recognize the necessity for comprehensive redevelopment. By comprehensive redevelopment I mean that which takes account of moral, political, and cultural problems as well as physical problems.... We in Pittsburgh have been inclined to do fire fighting, but not total redevelopment....
>
> We create an area-wide industrial development corporation for Western Pennsylvania. We finance it rather well and grace its Board of Directors with a blue-ribbon list of industrialists.... Yet our more effective leaders pass to the other side of the street when a public school problem appears. The plain truth is that public education does not occupy a high place in Pittsburgh's concern about redevelopment....

RYAN: True, the basis of this program was economic. But it takes more than pretty buildings or nice houses to attract people to a modern city—especially today's executives with their increasing cultural interests. So we have not neglected the noneconomic. For example, under the auspices of the Allegheny Conference, we set up the first real community educational television station—WQED. Today it is the only television station in the United States that is permitted to operate two channels in the same city. We have had the International Art Exhibit every two or three years, which has stirred up a little artistic controversy, to say the least. There is a citizens' commission currently studying the needs of the school system in the city of Pittsburgh; when they came up with some very strong tax recommendations, the Allegheny Conference appeared at the public hearing and went on record in favor of their proposals.

SNYDER: In addition, we acquired land in several spots and restored areas to be used for recreational purposes. And we sponsor the largest flower show in western Pennsylvania each year!

GROVE: One of the measures Governor Lawrence signed not long ago enables the city and the county to appropriate funds for Carnegie Institute for the Museum of Fine Arts. Like many of the nation's museums, ours represents a magnificent gift from Andrew Carnegie. But the funds to maintain the institution were not provided for, and, as costs have risen due principally to inflation, Carnegie Institute has had a difficult time.

MODERATOR BURSK: You mean to say that you have built up so much momentum behind this program that you can get hard-headed businessmen to support noneconomic pursuits with the same financial abandon and enthusiasm that they demonstrated on the economic projects?

LAWRENCE: They are not all the same people, of course; some are interested in one kind of project and some another. But we have been able to get backing. I should make clear that our primary objective is, and was, economic rejuvenation. Unless we can meet our needs in this area, we will be unable to do anything about the other, less material, one. But the point is that both are important and you cannot exclude either one from your community program.

The Businessman's Stake

What is the state of America's cities, and what is the business manager's stake in them? Are they really as badly off as Pittsburgh, and, if so, why should the business executive care? Mr. Babb opens the discussion of these issues with a dramatic statement:

BABB: Conditions are desperate in almost every city and town in the country.

MODERATOR BURSK: What do you mean by "desperate"?

BABB: There isn't a city in the nation which is free from the exodus of homeowners and businesses. Traffic has become so congested that people cannot get around quickly and easily, and companies cannot move goods smoothly. The central cities are unable to raise the funds to provide for all the necessary services like police, fire, schools, and so on.

What will happen tomorrow in view of the declining population and declining payrolls in the central cities?

LAWRENCE: You are 100% right. If you could attend the Conference of Mayors and listen to any mayor get up and explain his problems, you would find that all of them are running into these situations, and plenty of others besides. It is true that some of the newer cities in the West have not yet been hit quite as hard, but, believe me, their time is coming too.

BABB: The only difference in the problems in one city and those in another lie in the question of how old they are; not how wise they are but how old. The same process is taking place in every community, large and small, all over the country. People move from this house to another better one, and housing starts to deteriorate. Plants move from one location to another because one plant is old, and they go into a new one to have more room and easier access to markets, suppliers, and employees.[3]

So we get deterioration of physical property, movement of people, and congestion everywhere, in varying degrees. In those communities where it has not yet become a crisis, the citizens have an opportunity to do the redevelopment much more economically than those who have to tear down great areas of their central cities, or even vast sections of what is called the gray area, between the central business district and the suburbs, in order to get it back to being a good place in which to live and work.

[3] See the Linder case, p. 1.

MODERATOR BURSK: But for some reason it seems difficult to get insight and commitment and interest on the part of businessmen in the problems of their own home town.

BABB: Apparently they do not understand that the success of a business enterprise is often just as dependent on the economic climate in which it operates as on its internal management. We are concerned about the economic climate nationally, but our national economic climate is not going to be good if we have many communities, particularly the large metropolitan areas where most of the people live and work, declining economically rather than growing healthier.

A major part of economic climate depends on the very community in which the business has to operate, the way its people live, the services provided to them, their happiness, and their jobs. So the businessman, if he does not take care of the healthy development of his own community, is building a climate which ultimately is going to be detrimental to the interests of his stockholders.

LAWRENCE: Maybe the reason goes back to this business-versus-government phobia we mentioned earlier. The average businessman thinks politics and government are something that he should avoid, and he has to become involved in these areas in an enterprise like this. If he goes to City Hall he thinks he is going to be accused of butting in.

I do not think that is so. I think the average official today would welcome the businessmen of the community if they came in and said: "We want to pitch in and help the town. We are patriotic citizens. We are devoted to this community.

Our business is here, the people who work for us are here, and we want to help." But that step has to be taken in the community by the business leaders first. They cannot wait shyly to be asked.

MODERATOR BURSK: I am strongly convinced that there is a pretty fair number of cities across the country where the businessmen would not have quite the good luck with the operation in City Hall that the business community had in Pittsburgh, no matter how enlightened and anxious to do something they might be.

LAWRENCE: I suppose that is so anywhere—even in universities. Some do better than others, and in a few cities the best mayor in the world would be unable to gain business support. But, basically, my point is valid—and, anyway, the businessmen can always try to elect a mayor!

BABB: If the businessmen do not participate, the politicians are going to do this job by themselves. We all know what a red-hot issue this is now. People are not going to stand for slums and the kind of surroundings which they see in the downtown areas of this country. We are going to have action in this field, but whether the action is sound, in the economic best interests of the country, and efficiently carried out, depends on the participation of the business leaders of the community. If they want to let it go by the board, they are going to pay for it in their tax bills.

Furthermore, businessmen have special talents to contribute in this field. Most of the problems—not all of them but most—having to do with redevelopment of urban metropolitan areas are economic in nature, and require good organization for their solution.

The businessman is supposed to be somewhat experienced in both these fields. If he does not participate actively in the development of his own community, then the ignorant will be shapers of events.

LAWRENCE: That is entirely correct, and succinctly put. If the business people do not move in to do these things, they will not be done. It takes both the politicians *and* the business managers to move these mountains.

MODERATOR BURSK: Why don't more businessmen do it, then?

BABB: Why don't you ask *them*?

YOUR COMPANY AND POLITICS: SHOULD BUSINESSMEN RING DOORBELLS?

Editor's Note: The panel discussion on which this chapter is based centers around the Barlow Company case. The discussion was preceded by a short film, the script for which is presented here. Panel participants were: Don S. Greer, President of the J. W. Greer Company; William H. Lowe, Treasurer of Inland Steel Company; Thomas R. Reid, Manager, Civic and Governmental Affairs, Ford Motor Company; Sidney R. Yates, Democratic Congressman from the Ninth District in Illinois. Paul W. Cherington, the moderator, is Professor of Business Administration at the Harvard Business School.

FACT SHEET ON THE BARLOW COMPANY[1]

The Barlow Company is an old, established firm with assets of roughly $50 million and sales of approximately $65 million. In addition to its main plant in the Twentieth Congressional District of "Transylvania," it also operates a sizable plant in the Midwest and has several overseas subsidiaries. Approximately 18% of the Barlow Company's sales come from export, either to its subsidiaries or to distributors abroad. Although the company's direct sales to the government are relatively small, it estimates that approximately 24% of its domestic sales are defense-connected in one way or another.

Of the 2,100 production employees at its main plant in the Twentieth District, approximately 1,800 are members of a national industrial union. Most of the others belong to various craft unions. The company has had a union shop since the mid-1930's. In general it has enjoyed amicable relations with both the local and the national union officials, except in 1954 when a six-week strike over wages closed the plant.

Increasingly over the last ten years, the company has

[1] This is a case used at the Harvard Graduate School of Business Administration. Case material is prepared as a basis for class discussion, and cases are not designed to present illustrations of either correct or incorrect handling of administrative problems. The Barlow case was written by Paul W. Cherington and Dan H. Fenn, while the script based on the case was written by George W. Gibson. Copyright, 1959, by the President and Fellows of Harvard College.

placed its expanding production at its Midwest plant and its overseas subsidiaries. Thus, employment at the plant in Transylvania has declined somewhat. The Barlow Company management states that the buildup of production at the Midwestern plant was occasioned by the relatively high costs of doing business in Transylvania, but more particularly by the fact that Transylvania was far removed from many of the company's major markets. The Midwest plant, in this connection, was ideally located. In the fall of 1958, the company was considering the opening of a third plant located in the far West.

As a company, the Barlow organization itself has heretofore maintained a strict aloofness from politics. In 1952, and to a lesser extent also in 1956, two officers of the company were fairly active in the Republican campaigns for the Presidential election. These individuals, however, acted entirely on their own initiative and responsibility and, except for the fact that they were known to be officers of the Barlow Company, there was no linkage between the Barlow Company and the Eisenhower campaigns. One of these officers, Samuel Barber, the treasurer, was a member of the Transylvania Republican State Committee from 1952 to 1957.

The company belongs to a wide variety of associations, including the Associated Industries of Transylvania, the Greater Metropolis Chamber of Commerce, the United States Chamber of Commerce, and the National Association of Manufacturers. In addition, it belongs to several trade associations which serve the abrasives field.

*Scene I: The office of William Wheeler, presi-
dent of the Barlow Company. Wheeler and
Peter Blakeley, director of industrial relations,
are watching a television program.*

TELEVISION COMMENTATOR: And now to round out the WJX-
TV review of Transylvania's forthcoming statewide election, let's take a quick look at the situation in the Twentieth Congressional District. From this aerial view taken
one bright September afternoon of last week, it is hard
to get much of a sharp impression of the Twentieth. But
you can notice that to the northwest and west, the District
is largely residential, middle-class homes for the most
part, in the $17,000 to $30,000 class at today's prices. To
the southwest and east, there are several large and medium-
sized industrial plants. In between lies a belt of more
modest homes of industrial workers. That cluster of buildings over there is the plant and headquarters of the Barlow Company, a good-sized manufacturer of industrial
abrasives, grinding wheels, etc.

If you try real hard perhaps you can hear the sounds of
political strife from where you are sitting watching this
program, for the initial skirmishes of what promises to be
a hot Congressional campaign are definitely under way,
with William Sweeney, the Republican candidate, opposing Henry Ryan, the Democratic standard-bearer, in the
race to take over the post of the present Republican in-
cumbent, John Everett, who is retiring after 14 years
in Congress.

William Sweeney, the 49-year-old Catholic Republican candidate, is a native of the District. He is married, has four children, and runs a local insurance agency. Sweeney is a graduate of a nearby college and has served four terms in the legislature, three in the House, and one in the Senate.

His political record, according to the Transylvania Manufacturers' Association, has been "spotty" in that he has often voted "against" business interests and "for" labor interests. Nevertheless, Sweeney has the strong backing of the Republican State and National Committees.

His platform is essentially based on his support of the Eisenhower Administration. In a recent speech he outlined some of his views as follows:

SWEENEY (*appears on the screen, talking at a rally*): Though I agree with President Eisenhower in most of his policies, I do believe that United States foreign aid policy should be thoroughly re-examined. With unemployment at high levels in our own country, it seems only logical to feel that "Charity begins at home." (*Pause for applause.*)

During the last few months I have been the target of an increasing number of critics who say I have not always supported the Republican position at the State House or that my vote has been cast against business interests. To these charges I can only reply that I cast my vote as my conscience dictates. I am neither the creature of business nor of labor.

And now, ladies and gentlemen, let me conclude my remarks this evening by again reminding you that in the political arena as in all other forms of human endeavor, there is no substitute for experience. I know I need not dwell on the paucity of my Democratic opponent's qualifications in this respect. Suffice it to say, however, that the maturity and insight I have gained through the long years I have had the privilege of serving you in the Legislature of this great state of Transylvania will continue to be at your disposal if I am elected your next Representative to the Congress of the United States. I thank you. (*Applause.*)

COMMENTATOR: Here indeed is a situation that is worthy of your very close attention. On the one hand, we have the experienced, veteran politician and, on the other, a relatively unknown individual who must at least be rated as something of a dark horse. Henry Ryan, the Democratic candidate from the Twentieth District, is a 40-year-old political neophyte who is an honor graduate of the Harvard Law School and an alumnus of Harvard College. Like his Republican opponent, he too is a Catholic, married, and the father of four children.

After serving in the Navy, Ryan went to work as a lawyer for the National Labor Relations Board and quickly rose to be NLRB counsel in the Metropolis office before he went into private practice in that city in 1957. The law firm with which he is associated handles the labor-relations work for several manufacturing concerns in the Metropolis area, although some of the major ones, like the Barlow Company, are not their clients.

From here it looks as though this new contender for

political laurels can count on the backing of Transylvania's influential senior senator, who is himself a likely Presidential candidate on the Democratic ticket in 1960. This close association with one of the party hierarchy, plus the likely backing of the state AFL-CIO organization, may make Ryan very tough to handle come election-time.

Now, I don't want to give you the impression that this Twentieth District hopeful's campaign is going to be all "beer and skittles." Sweeney, the Republican standard-bearer, will make hay of the fact that Ryan has had no political experience. However, Ryan is already aware of this fact and in a recent speech said:

RYAN (*appears on screen in a press interview*): I admit freely to the charges of my Republican opponent that my record is devoid of actual "political" experience. Yet, on the other hand, I do not feel that legislative experience on a state level is any better qualification for the office of United States Representative than actual federal service. At least I am no stranger to Washington, D.C., or federal affairs as my many years with the National Labor Relations Board will bear out. However, it is not my intention to become drawn into a battle of personalities. Essentially I am running for office as a Democrat who will support "liberal" legislation, who will stand up for the protection of small business, and who will try to get a fair share of defense contracts allocated to firms in this District. (*Pause for applause.*)

Now we come to the subject of foreign aid. To begin

with, I must go on record as saying that, in general, I am
in sympathy with the position of the present Administration in this respect.

COMMENTATOR: There you have it, friends. You pays your
money and you takes your choice. And now this is your
WJX-TV political analyst, Steve Herrick, saying thank
you and good afternoon.

Blakeley shuts off the set and turns to Wheeler.

BLAKELEY: Bill, I purposely held off on this matter till today
so you could watch this show. I thought it would give you
a much more concise and up-to-date fill-in on this current
political situation than I could on such short notice.

Now—since Barlow Company policy is involved and
since you're the president, you'll have to pick up the ball.
So ... question: what do we do about Ryan's telephone call
asking for permission to tour the plant and address the
employees and the subsequent call from the union reinforcing his request?

WHEELER: That's a tough one to answer right offhand.
Ahh ...

BLAKELEY: Incidentally, I forgot to mention that I've already asked the union if they would favor letting the
Sweeney group in on the same basis and they said sure, to
go ahead if we want to.

WHEELER: Generous of them, wasn't it? But to get back to
your original question, Pete. Do you think we should
allow Ryan to tour the plant? If we do okay his request,

wouldn't that look as though we'd already taken sides, particularly since we aren't at all sure the opposition will ask for permission to do the same thing?

BLAKELEY: Well, it might. Yet on the other hand if we refuse, they could say we're interfering with the normal political process, particularly since they've okayed the idea of giving Sweeney equal rights.

WHEELER: Suppose we limited Ryan's appearance to the noon hour. Would that still look as though we were giving him an edge?

BLAKELEY: I'm not sure but what it might. After all, he would still be operating from company property with company permission.

WHEELER: Perhaps you're right. In any case, this isn't something I can decide right now. Maybe we can talk about it at the executive committee meeting tomorrow.

Scene II: A meeting of the executive committee of the Barlow Company. Present are Wheeler, Blakeley, vice president and treasurer Samuel Barber, sales vice president Paul Simpson, and manufacturing vice president Charles Nugent.

WHEELER: There's just one other matter we should consider before we adjourn. Since Pete has firsthand information, he might as well tell you about it.

BLAKELEY: Well, to be brief, the day before yesterday I got a request from Henry Ryan's political organization asking for permission to let him tour the plant and speak to the men during the lunch hour. Shortly after that, and somewhat coincidentally, the union requested the same thing. I talked briefly with Bill about it, and he felt it was a matter for the executive committee to decide.

BARBER: Does this mean that the company intends to depart from what has essentially been a neutral political position in the past?

WHEELER: Not necessarily, Sam. We're simply re-examining our position here, since it obviously will have a bearing on how we handle Ryan's and the union's requests.

BARBER: Fair enough. Now that the matter is open for discussion I've got a few things to say. To begin with, if the Barlow Company doesn't go along with the Republicans in this election we're making a big mistake! If businessmen don't get into politics—and soon—labor-dominated Democrats will get control of Congress, and by whopping majorities. Then the labor bosses will really call the turn. I don't need to tell you that that means more spending, higher taxes, soaring inflation, and absolutely no control over union activities. As far as I'm concerned, every executive of this company ought to spend the next two months working for the Republican Party. Now there's been a lot of talk going around that companies shouldn't get drawn into politics. Well, maybe they should and maybe they shouldn't, but that doesn't mean it's illegal for executives to work for candidates, even if they do it on company time!

SIMPSON: Well, I don't know. I don't want to see union

domination of the Congress, but I'm not so sure that that's what a Democratic victory would mean, especially in the light of the situation here in the Twentieth. I rather like the looks of young Ryan, and I must say that Sweeney leaves me cold, particularly his stand on foreign aid. That sort of thing could hurt our export sales.

Oh, I don't doubt Ryan will have union support, but this doesn't necessarily mean he'll do just what the union boys tell him to. We've always had a "hands-off" policy in this company in political affairs, and I think we should keep it.

Now if Sam wants to work for Sweeney, that's his business. On the other hand, if someone else wants to work for Ryan, let him. But let them do it on their own time. If we get involved, or if our executives are given time off to work for Sweeney, we'll be dead if Ryan wins. Or if Sweeney wins, the union will say we bought and paid for him. I feel we should maintain the status quo and keep the company out of politics.

NUGENT: Well, I more or less agree with Paul Simpson that we should keep the company essentially neutral. But I don't see why we can't adopt a policy where we encourage people as individuals to be politically active. The unions do this, but business doesn't take the initiative in urging the junior executives and white-collar people to lend a hand. So I think that as a rule of thumb we ought to make it clear that we encourage political activity regardless of party. Who knows—we might be able to generate quite a lot of support for Sweeney and the Republicans this way.

NARRATOR: After more discussion as to the general political policy that the Barlow Company should follow, Mr. Wheeler reminded the group that the immediate question still to be decided was whether they should let Henry Ryan, the Democratic candidate, tour the plant and speak to the employees during the noon hour. Then Wheeler asked the advice of the group, saying that he planned to defer until the next meeting any further discussion of the company's over-all political policy and respective merits, from the company's standpoint, of Ryan and Sweeney as individuals. [*End of script.*]

DISCUSSION

WILLIAM H. LOWE: It seems clear to me that the Barlow executives need to do three things:

(1) They should do some objective thinking as individuals.

(2) They have to hold some objective discussions of the problem.

(3) They have to determine what their goals are in this whole area.

SIDNEY R. YATES: I agree with Mr. Simpson of the Barlow Company. I like the looks of young Ryan, too, and I think that the executives of the Barlow Company should support him. He looks to me as if he can get along with the business community as well as with the labor unions.

But I don't think the company itself should support him. As a company it should not participate in politics at all. By the same token, labor unions as unions should stay completely out of elections. Legally, of course, neither union nor company funds can go for political purposes; but I would go beyond that and say that the company should not use its corporate influence in any way. I do think that the individuals in the company, just as I think members of labor unions, should participate to a maximum degree, as citizens. And I say this even though I have a hunch that, for the most part, the executives of companies like Barlow would not be working for the Democratic Party!

DON S. GREER: Whether they like it or not, the Barlow Company is in politics. Because they are caught unaware by this situation, they have to make a very important decision now which they should have been thinking about some time back.

Several years ago they should have considered what they were going to do about the general position of the corporation in the community's political situation. That they failed to do so is sharply brought home to them now by the fact that they are faced with an aggressive Democratic candidate and a weaker Republican one. If business doesn't get on its toes and do something to match this aggressiveness, it is going to continue to be caught short in election after election.

THOMAS R. REID: The case, as presented, is really only a scratch on the surface of a very deep problem for business. I am sure that the Barlow Company will realize this, too, as they discuss their situation further. Quite obviously, their present discussion shows they are too late with too little in dealing with government and politics. They are not going to change the direction of any trend at this stage, no matter what they do; they are not going to be effective at all at this late hour. Furthermore, they are completely confounded by a rather simple request, and find it necessary to go to the executive committee for a discussion of a question which should have been settled long before this.

All they can do is let this situation provide them the impetus to determine a policy and a program for the future. Mr. Ryan has done this company a great favor in calling their attention to an issue they should have thought of themselves a long time ago. But they don't see this yet. They have a piano to move, and they are worrying about how to lift the bench.

These men have to decide whether the impact of the government on the climate in which they do business is important to them or not. If they decide that it is—and more and more businessmen are doing so—then they must arrive at a policy not only with respect to partisan political activity, but on all governmental relations. Having arrived at the policy and determined what they propose to do, they must set up an organizational structure adequate to handle it as a part of their business operation.

As to the specific question—letting Ryan into the plant— their answer should be "no." There is no reason for political candidates to use company premises. Traditionally, political activities are conducted at the plant gates, and it should be kept that way. I certainly should hate to see American corporations faced with the equal-time dilemma of the communications media.

MODERATOR CHERINGTON: You all seem to agree that the Barlow Company should spend some time thinking about and discussing its objectives. What kind of objectives do you mean?

LOWE: One, for example, might be to get more Republicans elected. But when you think about that a bit, some troublesome questions arise. First, is it proper for a business organization to be partisan—aside from the legal restrictions involved? And second, how practical an objective is it? How can you measure your results, and what techniques are you going to use? If you try to impose a set of political views on people, are they going to take it out on you in some other way? We are all pretty sensitive about our right to hold our own opinions.

So it seems to me that Barlow has to aim for some other goal. To my mind, the best one is the improvement of the quality of government and government personnel at all levels. In the long run, this cannot help but benefit business —and all of us. This program is, of course, nonpartisan.

REID: I am a little dubious about all this nonpartisan activity to improve our governmental and political system.

GREER: Yes, I am concerned too when I hear the term "non-partisan." Don't we believe in the two-party system in the United States? Nonpartisan seems to me to be the wrong term; we are actually talking about "bipartisan."

MODERATOR CHERINGTON: All right, how does a company

like Barlow go about this business of "improving the quality of government"?

GREER: In two ways. First, they should do everything they can to get all of their people—and I don't mean just the executives but the people who belong to their unions as well —to get out and vote.

YATES: For whom?

GREER: For anybody. For whomever they want in any party.

YATES: For both parties? Fine.

MODERATOR CHERINGTON: If everybody should get out and vote for any party, doesn't this mean essentially, since nationally there are more Democrats than Republicans, that the Democrats would be favored?

GREER: Yes.

LOWE: The elections show it. Since 1952 it's been very clear.

MODERATOR CHERINGTON: So you are basically urging that the Barlow Company stir up a lot of Democrats to go to the polls?

GREER: There is a very large segment of the population which does not vote, a great many people who are too apathetic. The first job we have to do is to arouse more people to take an interest in politics and do something about it. Once we get them aroused so they will register and vote and become interested in politics, then business can convert them to its particular viewpoint. But you can't convert corpses. You've got to wake them up first.

Grass-roots organization is another way of improving government. True, both parties have some structure now, but they are rather indifferent and, at least in my experience, very ineffective. They need leadership. I would like to see some of the men in my company, both Democrats and Republicans, active in their local town committees where they can help step up the general interest of the population in political affairs.

By encouraging our people to do this job, we will improve the grass-roots organization, and get out a better and more intelligent vote.

MODERATOR CHERINGTON: Don, you have said that the company should encourage people to take an active part. Now, let's say that the Barlow Company puts out a statement to the effect that all employees are urged to work for and participate in the party of their choice. Suppose we have some middle-management people there—junior executives— who take a look at the top men in the Barlow Company. They readily see that these fellows are all strong Republicans. Are they apt to join in with the Democratic Party— if their leanings take them that way—on the strength of one mimeographed statement?

REID: Oh, it is going to take much more than a mimeographed statement to make this program come alive. But I suggest that as a good place to start. I believe that the Barlow Company should go on record with a declaration of policy which would be a guide to those who might have been concerned about even expressing Democratic ideas without permission. If the company issues a statement saying, "Yes, we do encourage your participation in the party of your choice," it eases the situation somewhat.

But such a document could become just a piece of paper unless Barlow follows it up with some action which proves that it really means it. If I were president of Barlow, I would assign some executive the responsibility for governmental relations and encouraging political activity by individuals, despite Barlow's small size. He would be the person who maintains the political relationships, becomes the source of guidance and direction for those who have questions on this subject, and keeps an eye on all the company's activities to spot any governmental actions that might affect it at the federal, state, and local levels.

If this step is taken, the company is saying, in effect, that this matter is of sufficient importance to require organizational provisions just as marketing and purchasing and manufacturing do.

MODERATOR CHERINGTON: Essentially, you think that this man could carry the ball for the company?

REID: He should be the coordinator of activities in this field. He should not determine policy stands; that job should be done by the appropriate people in top management. But he should provide the information and he should call specific issues to their attention. He should guide and direct the company's activity, and assess for top management the impact of various governmental actions upon the company. At the same time, he should be available to guide employees in this area, because cases will arise where an employee wants to talk to somebody about his particular situation.

Incidentally, if the top officers in the company are known as Republicans, it might be a good idea to give this job to a Democrat as an evidence of good faith. I know one firm that did so, and with good results.

MODERATOR CHERINGTON: Sid, suppose you were Ryan in this situation and you knew that the top management of the Barlow Company was working pretty actively for the Republicans. About six months after the election, presuming that you won, if they came to you and asked you to do something for them, what would your general reaction be? Would you do what they asked?

YATES: I think I would. Politics is different from business in this respect. If a businessman found that one of his subcontractors had been giving information to his competitors, he would probably get rid of that subcontractor—permanently! But the politician is likely to try to be of service to friend and foe alike for two reasons.

In the first place, as a practical politician, in this case I would do what I could to help Barlow in the hope that they might be with me in the next election—or, at least, that they might temper their opposition a little.

Secondly, I believe sincerely that once an election is over, a man represents all the people of his district without regard to party. This may sound naive. It may sound trite. But it's a fact, which I think most politicians accept. I understand that Don found this out with respect to a candidate of the

Democratic Party whom he opposed in a recent election. When he needed help later, he received it.

I might qualify this point of view by saying that any human being is quicker to listen to and help someone whom he considers a friend, or some person who has aided him in the past. I should also say that politicians, like anyone else, react to bitter, unfair, personal attacks; if Barlow's opposition to me had been vicious, I might be too angry to want to help them. But, under almost any circumstance, the door would be open to them.

This gives me a chance to say that I think we have a pretty good group of people in politics today. I wish that more of the business people of this country could come down to Washington and see the members of the House and the Senate of both parties. They would find men and women whom they would consider of the junior-executive type, possessing a great amount of idealism and a determination to represent the people of their district impartially. One of the worst mistakes businessmen make is to look down on politicians.

REID: I think this is true; they tend to be cynical, and scornful of both politicians and politics. Maybe this is what the psychologists call a defense mechanism. Maybe businessmen are a little envious and scared of the successful political leader.

If so, I don't know why. They are brave as lions in the face of the average business problem; why should they be timid as mice when they look at this one? It is a problem that affects their business operations, like any other. There is no reason why business people should stand back and lose the battle by default just because they are afraid somebody is not going to like what they do or say. Actually, people are going to respect you for speaking up for what you think is right—if it makes any sense at all. Maybe all this is a hangover from the depression days.

MODERATOR CHERINGTON: I have heard it said that businessmen simply are not very effective in politics because of the kind of people they are. Is this so—should Barlow executives stay out of this area, not only as candidates but as political workers, managers, treasurers, as well?

GREER: Though my experience has been comparatively recent in this field, my impression is just the opposite. There certainly is no reason why a man who can organize a group of people to get certain work done, whether selling a product or manufacturing it or promoting a service, cannot do an equally good job in getting people organized to put over an idea or to build up a political organization. Businessmen have been trained along these lines; they *can* work effectively and they certainly should.

YATES: I agree. I have had many businessmen working in my campaigns; they're good organizers and hard workers. My only objection is that I see many more of them in my opponents' campaign than in mine.

REID: I see no reason why companies shouldn't give training courses in practical politics, just as they give training courses in other fields. As a matter of fact, I think Barlow ought to undertake a program along these lines to help its men enter political work successfully. While they may have a few people who have proved effective in the past, they will need them in large numbers in both parties if they are to be represented adequately. Training is the only way to get this corps of workers. At the same time, it serves to develop an awareness of the importance of the field.

But I don't think this is the whole answer, and I am concerned when I see so many companies which seem to assume that if they offer training, they have done their bit. I believe Barlow should recruit volunteers for both parties among its middle-management people in both of its plants. The company could send out a card asking the employee to volunteer for work in his neighborhood for the party of his choice, to check off whether he is a Democrat or a Republican, and to send it back in. Then those cards could be tabulated and sent on to the party chairman concerned. And it is important to make sure that something is actually done later.

YATES: Suppose that a junior executive checks off the Democratic box on this card. Would his chances of advancement be as great as those who say they are Republicans?

REID: I would say yes, if his employers have any sense of citizenship whatsoever. If they do not, then heaven help us because we are in terrible shape.

YATES: But if the attitude of company managers is that the Democrats are against business, then this becomes something more than just a matter of personal taste. Won't they say "if this guy is a Democrat, he is against this company"? What I am really asking is: Can this effort to improve both parties and be bipartisan about it really have any meaning as long as key businessmen believe that the Republicans have all the good answers for them and that the Democrats are purveying all the evil? I don't expect anyone to be able to answer this, but I am worried that we may be kidding ourselves on this bipartisan matter.

LOWE: Now a related question: If Barlow is going to encourage these people to get into politics to improve the quality of elected officials, suppose one wants to run for office? Will you give him a leave of absence to run for office? And will you do so regardless of party?

For my part, I say yes, because if we don't we are simply mouthing some nice words about upgrading politics and not actually doing anything positive about it.

MODERATOR CHERINGTON: What about leave with pay?

LOWE: It would depend on the job he was to do, I would say.

MODERATOR CHERINGTON: You want to look at each situation. All right, let's say that somebody in the Barlow Company wanted to go out and help Ryan—not run himself, but help Ryan. Would you let him go for sixty days to help in the campaign?

LOWE: Sure.

MODERATOR CHERINGTON: On his time, or with pay?

REID: You are talking about an isolated situation. I have found that there aren't too many instances in political or governmental activity where it becomes necessary for a person actually to have time off from his job. If such a case occurs, let's rather draw the comparison with a man who becomes the chairman of the Community Chest campaign in his home town. In business, we consider that respectable. We seem to find a way to make services of that kind available. Why shouldn't we do the same thing to maintain representative government?

GREER: There is no reason why we shouldn't. There is a tremendous number of jobs and plenty of work to be done in local political organizations that can be best handled in the evening or after hours.

MODERATOR CHERINGTON: But just the same, this question of leaves of absence for candidates and for workers, with or without pay, affected or unaffected by the party or individual involved, is one that Barlow must face.

LOWE: I want to change the tack a little here and ask "why?" We've been talking about some of the hows—and we have dismissed the whys by saying that we want to "improve" government.

But "improve" means different things to different people. What don't we like? What do we want to change? What should Barlow want to see happen as a result of all this training and new executive activities and policy statements? Unless they have some real, specific purpose in mind, it seems to me they will be just stirring up a lot of dust—which may blow back in their own eyes.

YATES: Yes, what *does* business want to do? Haven't you already got a businessman's government in Washington? Do you want to change this administration now? You could go through the President's Cabinet and find plenty of businessmen in the executive branch running the government for the business community.

MODERATOR CHERINGTON: How about the Congress?

REID: And what about the lesser brotherhood all down the line? After all, we are not talking about the federal government alone, or a few individuals in state capitals. One of the obstacles to a clear understanding of this whole problem is the popular belief that the relations between businessmen and government consist of a few people going to Washington on appointment. Now, that's just not true.

Political and governmental activity is a volume operation. All the citizens of the United States are involved in it. And companies bump up against government at every level from local zoning changes to national tax legislation. When we keep that fact in mind, we discover that we are not discussing the actions or influences of a few individuals who happen to be in high office at the moment. We are asking whether business firms are willing to face up to the fact that corporate employees in recent years have virtually cut themselves off from day-to-day political activity, and thereby from influence throughout the governmental and political process.

This may have come about because the corporations have not encouraged such activity. It may even have come about because some companies have tended to discourage it. But whatever the cause, the time has come for American business to remind all of those who work for it that it is not only desirable but also highly essential to the preservation of

American government that they re-enfranchise themselves.

Whether it is the result of sins of commission or omission, somehow or other corporate employees, and particularly the so-called middle-management group—a sizable part of the electorate—have somehow gotten the idea that politics is regarded unfavorably by their employers.

Employers may not feel this way but people think they do, and this belief leads men to divert their energies into activities other than governmental and political ones. I suggest that the time has come for corporations, without getting into politics themselves, to say to their employees: "We believe that political activity is desirable and that you as individual citizens should work for the party of your choice just as you participate in charitable fund-raising drives and other community activities."

LOWE: Fine. But what do you mean by a corporation's staying out of politics? You mean that a company shouldn't have a Washington agent who goes and talks to the Congressmen—that it should be all individual, grass-roots stuff with no formal corporate representation?

REID: Governmental relations and political activities—I think the two are inseparable. But one aspect is dealing effectively with company problems relating to governmental actions and proposals, and the other is encouraging employees to become interested in political action as individuals.

LOWE: Like the chicken and the egg. If you are going to have good governmental relations, you have to spot good people and get them into the political process back here.

YATES: I would agree with Mr. Reid, also. But I think that the company should remember that there are plenty of men in public office in the Democratic Party like Governor Lawrence [2] whom the businessmen of Pittsburgh found to be an able public servant, one who could do the job and one with whom they could work. I don't think that the business community should state *ipso facto*—or believe—that the Democratic Party is the tool of organized labor and therefore slough it off, finding their only home in the Republican Party. So as long as you take that attitude, I think that you are going to be on the outside looking in.

REID: I don't take that attitude at all. Furthermore, I don't think that many who are associated with me do. This matter is considerably broader than either Democrat or Republican. It goes beyond minor disputes over whether all Democrats are bad and Republicans good. This is a question of representative government and of two broadly representative parties. Let the people decide. But be sure all the people do something about it.

MODERATOR CHERINGTON: Do you really mean to say that you don't care about issues and economic legislation—you just want to give democracy a hand? Don't you hope that *if* you stimulate all this interest and activity, new strength will be added to the conservative cause?

YATES: Yes, that worries me too, and that is why I was glad when Mr. Lowe asked why we are doing all this. Granted that you have all facets of political philosophy

[2] Mr. Lawrence is one of the contributors to this volume. See p. 29.

throughout your business community, the question that occurs to me, as an average politician, is: Whose voice is the
dominant one? Who is in the majority? Is the voice of the
business community the same as the voice of the people?

For example, I have a speech, given by William C. Stolk,
president of the American Can Company, that was inserted
in the Congressional Record by one of the Senators (May 20,
1959). In the course of the talk, he had this to say:

> You and I and other businessmen as corporate executives
> must give more personal attention to our unique opportunity
> to exercise the art of leadership, to fulfill our unique respon-
> sibility as managers of human resources. As corporate ex-
> ecutives, we have great opportunity to demonstrate and
> promote sensible ideas and constructive action for the com-
> mon good. Let me be specific: I believe that the economic
> realities and the social and political principles that have
> operated to achieve success for the American Can Company
> as a corporation are the same realities and principles that have
> operated to achieve success and prosperity for every employee
> in our business, in your business, and for every citizen.

In other words, what is good for the American Can Company is good for the country. I don't think that's necessarily
true. I think that there are many instances of conflict between what is good for the people of the country and what
may be good for any single corporation, or any other particular group. The whole challenge of a free government is
precisely in the reconciliation of clashing interests in order
to sustain the common good. When a business executive

seeks to equate the public good with the corporate good, he should re-examine his position—it is untenable. They may, of course, coincide briefly at some particular time and place, but they certainly will not do so all the time.

LOWE: I think I remember one fellow who went to Washington about 1953 and made the same mistake.

YATES: The Democrats got re-elected time and again because he made that comment. That's what I meant when I said that business was in danger of being locked outside permanently. People won't accept the idea that the interests of one group should be fostered above others, and they'll react strongly to it. They have come to realize that they, too, have a stake in their government; that certain segments of our community, including business, should be represented on all levels of the government.

MODERATOR CHERINGTON: I don't think that Tom Reid was arguing the case for a business monopoly in government.

YATES: Tom and I are not at loggerheads on this, but I am concerned about what seems to be the basic objective of the bulk of the business community. Furthermore, individual businessmen have tended to relinquish the expression of the "business point of view" to associations which too often reflect the desire for a monopoly, to use Professor Cherington's term. As a city member of Congress, the mail that comes across my desk expounds one absolute political philosophy from most of these associations.

When I talk to individual businessmen, they tell me, "That doesn't reflect my own viewpoint." For example, in this book a group of businessmen are writing favorably about the mutual-assistance program.[3] But most of my mail from business people is opposed to that program; they refer to it as a give-away.

MODERATOR CHERINGTON: This raises an important issue. Isn't it dangerous to talk about "the business viewpoint" when, in fact, executives hold a wide variety of views? Certainly the owner of the corner bicycle shop is going to look at reciprocal trade agreements very differently from the president of U.S. Steel.

GREER: For my part, I am not interested in seeing the business community have a monopoly on representation in the government—which would mean that it would control the state. But I don't want anyone else to have a monopoly either. And the thing that disturbs me is that an increasing segment of our population is being influenced by labor leaders and their philosophies, backed up by very large amounts of money applied with good organization right at the grass roots.

Unless businessmen make an effort to get an organization started to counter this power, our system will get even more out of balance than it already is. So when I say that businessmen should get into politics, I mean that they should help to organize at the grass roots. I don't care, myself, whether it's the Democrats that get out and work or the Republicans. If the company is headed by a Republican businessman, he will naturally encourage those in his organization who think

[3] See p. 89.

the way he does to get into politics, rather than those who disagree with him. The Democrats in business are naturally going to do the same thing. But the movement as a whole is bigger than any party issue.

LOWE: Nonpartisan but antiunion? Is that it?

GREER: Yes. If you feel strongly that the union people are taking over the country, I think it's perfectly proper to take an antiunion attitude. It would be equally proper, if you thought business was achieving the monopoly we've been talking about, to develop an antibusiness attitude. As a matter of fact, we've had one in this country for quite a while!

YATES: What is an antiunion attitude? For example, the labor unions are for public housing. Does this mean that the business community should be opposed to public housing? I don't think so; let me point out the fallacy here.

The contributors to another chapter in this book write about the necessity for urban-renewal programs to rehabilitate our metropolitan areas. But you cannot relocate the people who now live in these slum areas without providing some means of shelter for them. Most of these people do not have the incomes, do not have the financial resources, to buy housing on the market today. Therefore, if your urban-renewal program is to succeed, you must have public housing. Yet public housing is advocated by the labor unions— so this automatically means that it is bad, in your terms.

GREER: Not necessarily. But somewhere along the line we have to reach a decision on whether or not we can buy all of these projects. The danger, as I see it, is that one pressure group after another is advocating these various proposals. They want big airports; they want urban renewal; they want all kinds of gadgets. If we have people who are financially immature making these decisions in the legislatures, they are going to vote for every program that comes up, and we will finally find ourselves in a state of bankruptcy. So I say that businessmen who have had experience in staying financially solvent have some skills which they can bring to the public service to help redress the balance and determine how many of these fine luxuries we can afford to have.

Because businessmen have experience in meeting payrolls and in financial matters, they have the responsibility to help the public in general and politicians in particular to understand something about the balance between income and outgo. They have an obligation to halt this rush to national bankruptcy, this never-ending spending, spending, spending. This is not a partisan matter; actually if the businessman gets too partisan about it, he may find he has destroyed his effectiveness in doing what I think is an all-important task today. But it has to be done. I think the company must stay out of partisan politics.

MODERATOR CHERINGTON: Let's close this chapter with a quick recapitulation.

It is clear that all of us feel the Barlow Company faces an issue that goes beyond the simple matter of Ryan's request. The management should take a look at the firm's total relationship to government and politics. Some businessmen feel that they should view this relationship in terms of "corporate citizenship and responsibility"; others are concerned about the general "business climate"; and still others are anxious about what they see as the mounting power of labor unions.

I must say that I look at this problem a bit more pragmatically. I see no particular necessity for a business enterprise to ignore or disguise the fact that its self-interest is affected by governmental decisions. It seems to me that the executives of the Barlow Company would do well to look at the specific areas where it touches and is touched by government, from local zoning ordinances to federal tax legislation. They then can assess the importance of such measures to the company's well-being, and determine what kind of a political program would be best suited to creating and preserving the best possible governmental climate for them. In so doing, they should consider the long-range effect of the program on their various publics, establish standards of ethical conduct for their political dealings, and weigh the costs of such an undertaking against the possible gains.

I do not mean to say that all objectives other than specific company self-interest should be swept aside. The Barlow management might want to see what contribution, if any, it could make to improving the political process or the business climate. But I do believe that the place to start is with its own specific political interests and that any policy it adopts should be related to those interests.

YOUR COMPANY AND
THE WORLD AT LARGE

THE MERCK CASE

ON JANUARY 26, 1957, in Bangkok, Thailand, two officials of Merck Sharp and Dohme International, a division of Merck and Company, boarded a New Delhi-bound plane. One of

Note: This chapter is based on a panel discussion of the Merck case: an American company's experiences in an overseas operation. The contributors are: Roy Blough, Professor of International Business, Columbia Graduate School of Business Administration; James M. Fulton, Counsel for Merck Sharp and Dohme International Division; Don K. Price, Jr., Dean of the School of Public Administration, Harvard University; David Shepard, Executive Vice President and Director, Standard Oil Company of New Jersey. The facts of the Merck case which open the chapter are presented by Richard Robinson, Member of the Faculty, Harvard Business School. The moderator, Thomas H. Carroll, is Vice President of The Ford Foundation.

these men was James M. Fulton, Counsel for Merck Sharp and Dohme International, and a specialist in international-business legal problems. The other was Huskel Ekaireb, General Manager of Far Eastern and South African business for the Division, and a long-time resident of Asia.

New Delhi was to be the last stop in an around-the-world trip by the two men during which they studied general economic conditions and the position of their company's products in a number of Far Eastern and Southeast Asian countries. The trip had gone very well, but they feared that the problems to be confronted in India would be difficult to resolve—problems of government control, import regulations, and foreign exchange restrictions.

Instructions given to Messrs. Fulton and Ekaireb by the Merck management had been general. They were to explore how Merck might best maintain and improve its position in India in the face of mounting trade restrictions. Now, Merck had been importing its product into India for over 20 years and selling through two independent distributing organizations. In itself, however, it had manufactured nothing in India.

Early in 1956, the Indian government had announced its desire to manufacture streptomycin, a product commercially developed and manufactured by Merck. The Indians had asked Merck at this time to submit a patent and know-how licensing proposal. Antonie T. Knoppers, Vice President and General Manager of the Merck Sharp and Dohme International Division, had observed at the time that a license might preserve the company's position in India if related to an Indian manufacturing venture undertaken by Merck and an Indian company. Other Merck executives doubted the feasibility of the plan in view of the allegedly hostile attitude of the Indian government toward foreign and private enterprise.

Nonetheless, it had been decided that Ekaireb should look into the matter on his next trip, which followed shortly thereafter in mid-1956. He reported the Indian government's strong interest in working out the streptomycin license. But the Indians had seemed unwilling, he felt, to couple this arrangement with an authorization for the local private manufacture of other products, which is what Merck management desired. This development lay behind the visit to India in January 1957 by Fulton and Ekaireb.

Just as the two men boarded their New Delhi-bound plane in Bangkok, they were handed a copy of an address delivered three weeks before by A. Nagaraja Rao, Chief Industrial Adviser to India's Ministry of Heavy Industries. On this occasion, he had addressed himself to the expansion of the local pharmaceutical industry. Discussing his comments as their plane spanned the Bay of Bengal, Messrs. Fulton and Ekaireb agreed that Rao's speech contained both an opportunity and a threat. The opportunity was the list of drugs which the Indian government wanted produced locally under its second five-year plan. The threat lay in the news that a Soviet technical-assistance team was already waiting to advise the Indian government and to negotiate financial assistance for the development of an Indian drug industry.

On landing in New Delhi, the two men were met by Alfred J. Binder, technical adviser to Merck's Indian distributor, and probable general manager of any Merck enterprise in India. A major problem immediately discussed by the three men was how to link a Merck proposal to assist the Indian government in building a streptomycin plant and a Merck request for permission to undertake the private production of other drugs. Different officers within the government would act on these two matters, and it would be difficult to relate one proposal to the other in simultaneous negotiations. However, they found that the Indians themselves suggested a joint meeting to be attended by officials responsible for acting on both problems. Discussions commenced almost immediately.

With respect to the streptomycin project, the Merck group offered a technical-assistance contract to a government-owned corporation. For the production of certain other drugs and pharmaceuticals in which the company was interested, the three men proposed setting up a 60-40 partnership with the private Indian group, the 60% to be held by Merck. The reason for requesting majority interest, the three Merck officials explained to the Indians, was a desire to ensure management control over technical know-how, for, after all, the products would carry the Merck label. But at the same time, they believed that a substantial local interest was important from the very beginning in order to build into the enterprise a large element of mutual interest.

Eventually, the Indian functionaries asked: Would Merck be interested in a 50-50 venture with a government-owned development corporation to produce these other products? The Merck representatives admitted that they did not know how their management would react but that they would certainly be willing to discuss the idea. And on this note the meetings terminated.

The three Americans realized that the Indians with whom they had been talking were anxious, apparently, to reach some sort of an agreement with Merck. Nonetheless, the Indians were under pressure, it was felt, from some of their own people to accept proffered Soviet aid for the development of streptomycin and other pharmaceutical-chemical manufacturing. If the Russians succeeded in reaching an agreement with the Indian government in this respect, it might well mean that the entire industry would be thrown into the public sector, and Merck and all other producers would be out permanently. It was understood that the Russians were offering a $25 million, 40-year loan at 2% interest to finance several basic units for the pharmaceutical-chemical industry, including a streptomycin plant.

But, on the other hand, was Merck really justified in helping the Indian government build a state-owned enterprise? And how far could the Indian government be trusted not to move in on any private venture in which Merck might become involved? And should cold-war political considera-

tions enter into a management's decision anyway? At any
rate, Merck International Division sounded out the opinion
of executives of other American companies with Indian interests as to what the technical-assistance contracts were for
investments in India at this time. Opinions varied widely.

Eight months later, in October 1957, after a good deal of
research and discussion at home on the part of the company's top management and directors, Merck International
Division submitted a formal package proposal to the Indian
authorities. Its main features were these:

(1) Merck would construct in the private sector a multi-
purpose medicinal-chemical plant.

(2) Merck would make available to an Indian government corporation—Hindustan Antibiotics, Limited—its
know-how, technical assistance, and patent rights with respect to streptomycin, dihydrostreptonaycin, and penicillin.

(3) Although not interested itself in manufacturing vitamins other than B_{12} in India, Merck would provide know-
how and technical assistance in respect to these other products.

(4) Merck would participate in the ownership of an Indian company to manufacture pharmaceuticals in order to
be assured of a reasonable share of the pharmaceutical market for its own labeled and formulated material.

Now it should be noted here that the idea of a joint-
ownership venture with an Indian government corporation
had been, after much thought, rejected by the Merck management because of the inherent and basic conflict of interests believed to be involved between the two prospective

partners. The relationship with the government corporation had to be limited simply to a licensing association.

On receipt of this proposal, the Indians expressed some disappointment and invited the Merck representatives to return for further discussions. Shortly thereafter, *Business International* published a report from its New Delhi correspondent to the effect that the Russians had, in fact, made a deal with the Indians. On the same day that this item came to the attention of Merck management, another letter from Rao arrived in New York. He indicated that the Indian government was still very much interested in reaching some sort of agreement with Merck. The upshot was that a Merck team was dispatched to India in February of 1958 for a second round of negotiations. In the ensuing negotiations, Merck made three important concessions:

(1) The company agreed not to make the government-licensing project depend on receipt of permission for the private manufacturing project. The Indians promised, however, to do the best they could for Marck in securing the necessary permits for the private project.

(2) Merck waived any initial cash fee for its know-how.

(3) Merck agreed to a minimum royalty whether the private manufacturing project was approved or not.

And Merck also agreed to assist the Indian government in finding dollar financing to cover the purchase of equipment needed for the streptomycin plant, which would be constructed by the government corporation. The Indians were delighted, and an agreement was reached on this basis.

Thus, in April 1958, Merck signed a 10-year patent and technical-assistance contract with the state-owned Hindustan Antibiotics, Limited, for the manufacture of streptomycin and its derivative, dihydrostreptonaycin. (Antibiotics, Limited was already producing penicillin.) The Americans promised engineering assistance for plant construction, technical assistance for production, the use of Merck patents and improvement information on the two products, and related manufacturing processes for a period of 10 years. In return for the improvement information and continuing technical assistance, Merck was to receive a fee equal to 2½% on sales in India and 5% on sales outside India, such payments to be made in United States dollars.

And a month later, in May, Merck secured permission to establish a privately owned Indian corporation to produce a line of Merck pharmaceuticals and certain medicinal chemicals. Private Indian interests would hold a 40% interest. Merck's investment would total $3.5 million.

Now, several important questions are raised by Merck's experience in India. Among these questions are these:

First, are American free enterprise concepts necessarily valid under all times and all circumstances? More specifically, are there good reasons for direct government participation in developing India's pharmaceutical industry?

Second, is it possible for private American firms and agencies of foreign governments to establish mutuality of interests within the context of jointly owned enterprises?

And, third, how much should managements be influenced in their decisions by the fact of the cold war?

SOME STATISTICS ON MERCK & CO., INC.

Sales and Earnings Information

Net sales during 1956 for Merck and subsidiaries totaled $172.4 million; net income, $20.2 million; working capital, $73.4 million; net fixed assets, $63.6 million; total assets, $168.0 million (including $8.7 million in Canada and $16.4 million overseas). The company's operating results for the year were the best in its history, sales rising 9% and net earnings 18% over those recorded in 1955.

Merck Organization

The company was formed in 1953 with the merger of Merck & Co., Inc. and Sharp & Dohme, Incorporated. It is divided into five divisions: Merck Chemical Division; Merck Sharp & Dohme Division; Merck Sharp & Dohme International Division; Merck & Co., Ltd. (Canada); and Merck Sharp & Dohme Research Laboratories. As of 1956, it was operating seven plants in the United States, two in Canada, and ten overseas (Argentina, Australia, Bermuda, Brazil, Colombia, Holland, Mexico, Philippines, and two in England). The International Division was responsible for export sales and the management of all foreign subsidiaries except the Canadian.

Merck Products

Chemicals and drugs, principally for use in the pharmaceutical industry; products for animal health and nutrition; vitamins and other products for the food industry; and a wide range of chemicals for industrial use. The firm engages in extensive research.

Products Involved in Proposed Indian Venture

Vitamins B_1, B_2, B_6, B_{12}, C, and K; pantothenic acid; the steroid hormones; cathomycin, streptomycin, dihydrostreptonaycin; and penicillin.

Indian Government Policy

In April 1956, the government of India declared a new industrial policy. Declaring a "socialist pattern of society as the objective of social and economic policy," the statement classified industries into three categories. Category one included those whose future development would be the exclusive responsibility of the state. Category two consisted of those industries which would be "progressively state-owned" and in which the state would, therefore, "take the initiative in establishing new undertakings" but in which private enterprise would be expected "to supplement the effort of the state." All remaining industries were assigned to category three, the future development of which would "in general be left to the initiative and enterprise of the private sector." Products of interest to Merck fell within category two.

Miscellaneous Statistics on India

Population: 392,440,000 (est. July 1957)
Occupation: 70% of population dependent on agriculture
Literacy: 25% of the population over ten years old (est. 1956)
Per capita income at current prices: Rs 289 (U.S. $60.70) in 1957–1958
Change in real capital income: 1951–1956, up 11.1%
                               1956–1957, up 3.6%
                               1956–1958, down 2.8%

DON K. PRICE, JR.: The case involved in this chapter is simply a business situation involving business decisions. And yet in another sense—and no businessman fails to feel this when he gets in today's world east of Suez—it is a most important issue in a game the stakes of which are, not to overstate the matter, civilization as we know it.

The great shock that a businessman—or any representative of a private agency—feels abroad comes from the clash between some of the values that he takes for granted and the connotations that these same beliefs have in the minds of the people with whom he is dealing. To put it bluntly, in India and in most of South and Southeast Asia, it is a political truism that capitalism is a dirty word. It is our political institutions (which the businessman does not generally view with pride), and not our economic ones, that are being widely imitated and admired in the underdeveloped countries today. And the great problem that any of us have in doing business of any kind in that area—commercial, industrial, governmental, or philanthropic—is how to bridge this fundamental gap between minds and points of view.

Underlying this disagreement over the term "capitalism" is an equally pronounced conflict of assumptions on the nature of the American business system. The image of American business held widely in the underdeveloped countries is one that had some validity in about 1880, but which bears only the slightest resemblance to today's complex economic machine.

Though we have learned a great deal in the last 75 years about the nature of our own economic institutions and have modified them profoundly, most Asians do not realize it. For example, the extent to which the American businessman works in community institutions and trade associations, and in collaboration with governmental agencies, and the degree of dedication to public service which is built into his business decisions have virtually escaped the notice of his Asian colleagues. Only a considerable period of common cooperation is going to persuade them that it really happens.

Meanwhile the American businessman has to understand

the nature of economic problems as they actually appear in the underdeveloped countries, and the fact that our clichés about them do not fit any better than theirs do about us. Just as our missionaries found out how little their local cultural background and denominational differences meant in dealing with the great mass problems of poverty that they faced, so we must look at the objective situation in these lands rather than simply the devices they employ to handle them. This is especially true in the area of the relationship between government and business.

We should not find this very difficult; all we have to do is stop and think what a large proportion of our own free enterprise is intimately associated with some sort of governmental program. Look at our defense budget and all the free enterprise that has grown out of that bit of governmental policy which implements a national objective; then think about the dominant purpose of a country like India which is determined to catch up in a few short years, if possible, with endless needs of health and nutrition and the other fundamental demands of existence itself. Considering the similarities here, it ought to be relatively easy for us to forgive them for not conforming to the precise patterns that we are used to in this country—or that we were once used to and are now changing, almost unconsciously, as we go along. For we, like the less-advanced nations, have established national goals which demand extensive public—or governmental—action and participation in the economy. Yet in both instances the importance of the end in the minds of people overrides the untried or untraditional means being employed.

Viewed against this background, it is clear that Merck showed considerable statesmanship in its willingness to work out some practical cooperative relationships on a pragmatic and sensible basis still within the basic context of free institutions. The distinction between free and slave institutions is, of course, the fundamental one. All other issues drop away when you get in an area like this where the chips are down. But the framework is a wider one than we sometimes realize and leaves us much more maneuverability than we think. For the American corporation, the basic question about the government is not whether some of its catch-words are socialistic and some of its institutions involve government ownership. Rather, business fears the lack of basic stability more than anything else.

Merck reaped the great benefits of more than a century of Indian experience in the development of a trained civil service. Taught by the British, acknowledged masters in the business of training for civil service, the hope of India today is that the stability supplied by those institutions will make possible the growth of a modern kind of business freedom, although under catch-words that are going to be unfamiliar to us.

I should point out here that India is an outstanding exception to the general rule in this regard. When you consider the whole range of underdeveloped countries, particularly in South and Southeast Asia, you are dealing with nations governed by men who have had very little training in the processes of government. Indonesia is one of the most striking examples: A few years ago on my only visit there, I was told that there were only a couple of dozen native Indonesians who had been graduated as engineers by the time Indonesia became independent. When you duplicate this situation in the rest of the professions and business and government, you do have to fear socialism or communism. Even more, however, you have to fear a complete breakdown in the machinery of civilization which is necessary to support a business enterprise.

Finally, the American businessman has to work out and accept new relationships with his own government if he is to conduct business in underdeveloped countries. So far, we have not had much success in the development of these patterns, and the government, on its part, has not provided adequate leadership. Until we begin to spend the same amount of money and imagination in training a public servant for duty abroad as we spend in training a monkey we send up in a space missile nose-cone, we are not going to be prepared for the job that faces us as a nation.

DAVID SHEPARD: The case presented has a great many aspects that are worth observing and discussing. I choose two on which to concentrate: the importance of economic soundness as distinct from the philosophical attractions of a project in international business, and the questions—at least a few of them—associated with governmental controls applied to private business investments in many countries.

First, then, the importance of economic soundness. I suppose from a businessman writing for an audience of managers, the mere mention of the precept is sufficient. I shall not, therefore, belabor the point for long. But I would not feel comfortable without emphasizing my conviction that sound character, economically speaking, is the first essential to the success of any business enterprise anywhere.

If this quality is lacking, then the enterprise would not retain the physical health over the long term to keep an area of commercial activity from falling into what has been called the "public sector." No private commercial venture can suffer long-term damage through economic frailty and still retain enough vigor over a sufficient period of time to hold the business in the private sector and thus avoid the inefficiencies and other disadvantages which the businessman sees in government-operated manufacturing enterprise.

The second area which I want to mention is that dealing with government controls on private businesses. Of course, some such controls, like taxes and antitrust laws, are regulations of long standing, and are basically well accepted, however much the businessman may grumble. But the extravagant growth in weight, number, and variety of fiscal regulations of government can turn a profitable operation into an uneconomic one overnight.

Price controls or profit limitations, foreign exchange controls, restrictions on the employment of expatriates, limitations on freedom of choice for management as to what goods to manufacture or not to manufacture—all these are examples of governmental controls which an investor in foreign fields must consider. Whether such controls are applied, and the degree to which they are imposed, may greatly endanger management's control of an enterprise. As in many fields, a judicious balance is the condition to be sought.

When that happy medium is maintained, the American investor abroad, the host government, and the people of the host country all profit. But if the government errs in its judgment of how many golden eggs the goose can lay, or if mutual confidence is destroyed by failure on either side to stick to its agreements until mutual—not unilateral—decisions or modifications are made, then benefits for the investors, governments, and the ordinary people concerned may well vanish.

Since capital, whether it be private capital or the taxpayer's money used by government, flows into new investments because it is attracted to do so—not because it is forced to do so—the present and projected circumstances under which the investments will exist are vital. The kinds of government controls and the character of the government now and in the foreseeable future obviously deserve the most careful scrutiny by the investor. Those controls can permit or prohibit a successful enterprise.

As Mr. Price wrote in his comments, the kind of stability which gives you some guarantee of where your business is going to be tomorrow, stability that is predictable in its

essence, is a matter of vital importance to any company.
Merck had that stability; therefore it was able to make the
unusual arrangements which it established in India.

ROY BLOUGH: In this case, Merck started with a strong
sympathy—at least it exhibited a strong sympathy—for the
viewpoint of India. The patience which the negotiators
showed does not come through clearly in the brief summary
presented with this chapter, but it was considerable. Out of
this combination of sympathy and patience came a workable
agreement.

This agreement involved a joint venture: a proposed joint
venture with the government and an actual joint venture
with private interests in India. Consequently, I would like to
focus my attention on this device as a method of bringing industrialization to underdeveloped countries.

Industrialization has to come from where it is, and that,
of course, is largely in the private enterprise of Europe and
the United States, although in the Soviet Union there is
some industrialization to be had for a price. The mechanics
of getting this industrialization from one area to another
have been complicated, and have precipitated disagreements.
United States firms in general, for instance, have preferred
to go into countries with branch operations or wholly owned
subsidiaries, while it is probably true that the underdeveloped
countries themselves would really prefer to be able to borrow
from governmental bodies or, failing that, through private
portfolio investment. They would then hire the technology,
the know-how, the management, and the training, either for

cash royalties or a minority stock interest, and keep control of the situation themselves locally. Japan has come closer to this system than any other country.

But very often this approach is not feasible, and the joint venture has been proposed as a method of meeting the interests of both parties. The host countries like it, in part because they want to gain prestige through the control of their own industries. Furthermore, they want to keep as much of the profit at home as they can. Finally, they feel greatly put upon by colonialism and so want to be especially sure that local workers and managers will be trained rather than exploited in the nineteenth-century sense.

American companies vary widely in their attitude toward joint ventures. These differences arise partly from experience, partly because of the industry involved, partly out of personal predilections, and partly from the attitudes of top management toward the underdeveloped world and our responsibilities to it.

Some companies declare they will never undertake such a project in an underdeveloped country with any local organization, governmental or private. Some of them have been burned, and their managers speak very firmly from this experience. Of course, after these particular men have departed from their company's organization, the firm's attitude may change. Other companies accept joint ventures reluctantly but insist on majority control. And still others welcome them and accept, sometimes even prefer, to have only a minority interest.

The companies that favor joint ventures see very positive values in these arrangements. In a European country, for example, they may get an exchange of know-how; in either a European or an underdeveloped country, they may get a distribution mechanism. In some instances where the international division of the company is not very well supplied with money by the directors at home, the only way to set up shop is to use local capital. To hear the international division people talk, you would be surprised how narrow-minded directors in domestic companies are about international operations. In addition, the joint venture eases the pathway to local acceptance. It is not easy for a foreigner to be taken in as part of the local industrial scheme anywhere, but it is important. This acceptance is particularly significant in doing business with the government, and especially tricky in that the government's attitude toward your business must be such that if a political change takes place you will not suffer. The best way to accomplish this end is to introduce local people into your structure in important posts.

But in the final analysis the compelling reason for joint ventures in most cases is that the companies involved cannot avoid them. They must either work out some such plan, or they do not get into the foreign country at all. Under those circumstances, they must make a calculation and decide whether something is better than nothing.

There are, of course, real problems involved in joint ventures. To begin with, it is usually hard to get the capital locally when the business is starting and is still a risky venture. Later, when the business is a success and the United States company can easily get local capital, it tends to lose interest in the joint venture approach. After all, the project has worked out well on a wholly owned basis; why should the American company want to cut anyone else in?

Conflicts often arise over management principles. For example, the family is the dominant feature of many businesses in the underdeveloped world, and consequently nepotism is considered good rather than bad. Again, attitudes toward relationships between the managers and their employees may be quite foreign to our ideas.

Or policy differences with regard to matters like pricing may develop. The United States company, in general, wants a promotional price set fairly low at the beginning, and is willing to forego a profit the first year or so in order to lay the groundwork for the future. The local people, on the other hand, may resist this, being well satisfied and happy with a high mark-up right from the start, planning on high prices, small volume, and short-term profit.

The impact of governments on management may be extremely taxing and, in our eyes, even bizarre. In some countries governmental officials may even go so far as to insist that the joint venture company hire certain employees for political reasons.

Finally, the foreign managers may well have a different attitude toward profit accumulation from the United States interests. We are likely to try to make the investment dollar stretch by reinvesting the profits. The American directors at home do not care if you bring your money back right away; they are not going to give you any more, but they will let you use what you make. So our managers want to plow the profits back in. The local partners, however, are used to taking cash out; many of them have to live on their earnings. In any event, they traditionally do business this way and are unfamiliar with any other approach.

These are not the only problems which enter into the picture, of course, but I have listed enough to indicate that joint ventures are not all sweetness and light. Nevertheless, I am convinced that the best solution to the problem of industrializing underdeveloped countries lies in this technique, and the significance of the Merck case is that it provides an excellent guide for the rest of us.

JAMES M. FULTON: The purpose of our two trips to India was to locate and to try to work out an economically justifiable arrangement which would be of mutual benefit to the host country and to us. Our basic objective was not to fight the Russians, though that aspect did ultimately creep into the picture, adding a considerable amount of spice and excitement to our negotiations. I suppose we have to consider the conflict with the Russians in underdeveloped areas as virtually an inherent part of doing business there.

I do not mean to say that we had not thought of the implications beforehand. The company recognized that drugs and pharmaceuticals were and would be of social and political significance to India. We were also well aware of the significance of India to the free world, and of the struggle

YOUR COMPANY, THE WORLD AT LARGE

between Russia and the free world for the allegiance of India. These circumstances injected a higher degree of urgency into the picture, to be sure, but the point is that our primary business is drugs, not international politics, and we mean to keep it that way.

The cold-war implications of business abroad, however, do make some particular policies advisable even though they do not ordinarily apply. I would like to turn my attention to several of these. In the first place, we worked closely with the Departments of State and Commerce in Washington from the very beginning. In addition, during both our trips to India, we worked with and through the United States Embassy in New Delhi. We found it very helpful to discuss day-to-day developments in detail with Ambassador Ellsworth Bunker and the members of his staff. Based on our experience, we believe that it is most important for industry and government to work as closely together as possible, particularly in the less-developed areas of the world.

In our case, the instructions from the company, particularly on the first trip, were very general in nature. We knew that we would have to come up with a proposal which would be appealing to the Indian government as well as to our company if we were to be successful. So we had no precise preconceived notions when we went, and that fact alone proved to be very important to us. We were able to be flexible in our thinking, and to adapt to India's needs and desires as expressed by Dr. Rao. Since the final plan had to be *mutually* agreeable, our principal mission was to understand the situation as the Indians saw it and work out a program. If we had been given precise orders by the company, it would have been far more difficult for us to fit together a workable scheme.

American business should recognize fully the significance of the impact it makes on the host country. To help, it has recently formed the Business Council for International Understanding. This nonprofit organization, under the leadership of top business people, has developed a program to improve business representation abroad, to work more closely with the government both here and overseas, and to set up affiliates in foreign countries that will enable United States firms there to participate in broad economic and social programs for the betterment of their adopted lands. Two such affiliates are already operating in Mexico and Colombia. This development represents an encouraging start. However, much more needs to be done.

No one should expect the Russians to lie down after losing an initial skirmish like ours. Even though our company in India is organized, its staff being built up, and production started for some of the products in leased quarters, the brush-fire keeps burning. The Indian government and Merck have both been strongly attacked by the Communists in India and in the Indian parliament. These assaults were beaten back, and the Indian government was able to justify the contracts we entered into with it. In the meantime, the Russians have continued their negotiations and, according to the latest reports which we have received, a team from the Indian government has been in Moscow negotiating with the Russians on a proposal for Russian technical and financial assistance to build facilities for the production of a very large number of medicinal and other chemicals in India. There will certainly be many more chapters in the history of the struggle with the Russians in the pharmaceutical and chemical field in India. It will be a long war, and these encounters of ours should be recognized as nothing more than an early beginning. No one can settle back and consider a job done even though the first part of it may have been successfully concluded.

Finally, American business is going to have to be alert to the possibility that we will have to make some legislative changes at home if we are to compete successfully with the Russians. One example, which struck me especially during our negotiations, is in the antitrust field.

While it may be reassuring to hear statistics on the relative efficiency, production capacity, technical ability, and whatnot of an American industry as compared with a similar industry in Russia, it is also very misleading as far as an individual company goes. When we were in India, for instance, we were representing only one company with its products and its skills. We did not have available to us all of the products, technical skills, financial strength, and the like, of the American pharmaceutical industry. This same limitation would apply to any other American company or industry.

But it is not true, of course, of the Russian government

nor, in fact, of industry in the rest of the countries of the free world where cartels and business arrangements are allowed and, indeed, in some instances encouraged. Such operations are prohibited to American industry because our antitrust laws are applicable to the conduct of business outside of the United States. In any competition with Iron Curtain countries today, the American company essentially has to go it alone. And this is a fact which must be taken into consideration in assessing our strengths and weaknesses in this struggle.

You will notice that I said, *"essentially* has to go it alone." Organized industry can properly do a lot more in the way of sharing experiences and knowledge of the problems of doing business or establishing a business in foreign countries. For example, the Pharmaceutical Manufacturers Association has established an International Section which devotes itself entirely to legal, financial, engineering, personnel, and similar problems in foreign countries. Furthermore, for our part, we received a great deal of very valuable and helpful advice from American companies in other industries, particularly from some of the oil companies, based on their knowledge and experiences in the Far East.

But it may well be that this informal cooperation will not be enough. Recently, in this connection, the President's Committee on World Economic Practices has recommended that the Mutual Security Act be amended so as to authorize exemptions from the overseas applicability of the antitrust laws where the arrangement or agreement has either been requested by the President or has been approved by him or a delegated official as being in the public interest. The business community should seriously consider backing this kind of measure.

To return, however, to my first point: to me, the primary lesson to be learned from an experience is the advantage of the positive approach. While the competition with the Russians provided most of the excitement and is of great significance, our basic purpose was a business one. We were trying to find out what India needed and wanted, and how we, as an American private company properly concerned with the long-range profitability of any venture, could help fill these needs and grow with that country.

It is only because we found the answer to that problem that we were able to come to agreement with the Indian government and were able to succeed to the extent that we did in this first skirmish with the Russians.

BLOUGH: There is one important aspect of this case which we have not mentioned: the long-term nature of the Merck commitment. They were not thinking in terms of 90 days or a year or two, but of 10, 20, 30 years or maybe even longer.

This kind of investment in an underdeveloped area demands that you make calculations of risk, including the possibility of political instability. Now, clearly, there is hardly an underdeveloped country that is not going to go through some fairly major political upheaval during the next 25 or 30 years.

On the face of it, this sounds discouraging. But history

gives us some assurance that this is worrisome from the long-range point of view only if it results in a communist take-over. Thus far, this is the one political change that has proved to be irreversible. Actually, aside from a successful communist revolution, political instability can well be followed by political stability which will require some re-negotiations and involve some harm, but which will not preclude profitable American business. So it seems to me that the shrewd manager will plan for this kind of eventuality, and be prepared to handle it, financially and otherwise, if it comes.

SHEPARD: I disagree in part, because I find political instability very worrisome indeed. But basically you are entirely correct when you say that many American concerns doing business outside the United States over a long period have been through many a political upheaval. And, in retrospect, one can see that by and large the curve has continued to be in the right direction in spite of the political upheavals, difficult as it may have been for the American enterprises at the time.

MODERATOR CARROLL: Professor Blough made a very strong case for the joint venture in his comments. I know that when Mr. Fulton was working on this problem he had some very vigorous discussions in the Merck Company about it.

FULTON: The company had always anticipated that we would go into this venture with an Indian private company as partner, and this, of course, was the final conclusion. The company felt that if we were going into a country like India we needed somebody who knew the area and would have a local interest. Then I suppose we thought that eventually we would have to participate in a joint venture. We saw that it might be forced on us, and if we were going to have to marry the girl someday, it was better to do it now and do it gracefully!

However, during our first visit the Indian government did ask that the company consider going into partnership with a government-owned corporation. This question, as Mr. Carroll has pointed out, led to some very vigorous discussion in the company and stimulated a lot of thinking.

Some believed that there were real advantages in such a joint venture, even with the many difficulties. They also felt that the complications were not as great as might be thought on first consideration. For example, these enterprises are organized as private companies with the government as stockholder; the board of directors expects the company to make a profit; and the company pays the same income taxes as any other private company. If a government bureau or department wants to buy something and finds it can get it cheaper from a private company, they will buy from it. I do not say that it will always be that way, but these are the rules now.

As to the problems of government involvement and regulation, we were not sure that even the exclusively private firms are free of them in a country like India. The government has so many regulations that they are virtually participants anyhow; they are either under the table or across the table from you in any negotiations. Everything is very closely controlled, and you cannot manufacture anything you want to in the way you want.

The final top-management recommendation, which was concurred in by the board of directors, was that we not enter into partnership with the Indian government corporation. Fundamentally, we felt that there would inevitably be a basic and continuing conflict of interest between a private company with profits as one of its important motivations and government primarily motivated by social and political considerations.

CONCLUDING COMMENT[1]

On a recent trip to the Middle East, South and Southeast Asia, and the Far East, the vital questions posed in this chapter struck me with great force. Over and over, in country after country, I asked myself: "What can an American business firm do abroad—especially in a lesser-developed country—in order to persuade the people that American private enterprise can contribute significantly to their nation's economic development? How can we show them that they need not resort to totalitarian methods in order to raise their standard of living?"

John T. Connor, president of Merck and Company, whose Indian venture served as the focus of this Chapter's discussion, has stated the challenge in most provocative terms:

[1] By the moderator, Thomas H. Carroll.

Let us remember that some people in this world have a hard time believing that the American corporation deserves a major share of the credit for the social benefits and the high standard of living that we enjoy in the United States. They have known businessmen mainly as traders and exploiters, which is perhaps part of the explanation why so many countries have turned to socialism. If we can perform as well in the underdeveloped countries as we have at home, and do it with humility and with understanding, perhaps we can persuade them that we have found a way of improving the welfare of their citizens that makes socialism obsolete.[2]

The American oil industry has had unusually extensive experience overseas. Upon sober thought, most American business and governmental leaders would agree, I believe, with the assessment of the international mission assumed by American business enunciated by one of that industry's able spokesmen, Theodore S. Petersen of the Standard Oil Company of California, in a talk delivered at a private meeting in New York City recently. First, he says, its job is to run successful businesses, to make money, without which other useful objectives cannot be achieved. Second, it should help develop the natural resources of the less-advanced free countries, so that their economies will be bolstered and these precious raw materials will be available for the continued economic progress and security of the entire free world.

[2] "An Early Skirmish in the Global War against Diseases," talk delivered at an East-West briefing session of the American Management Association, New York, November 6, 1958.

And, third, it must embrace as an objective the strengthening of the economic underpinnings of free countries and thereby advance both the progress and the military security of all free nations, including our own.

What we need particularly is a fuller appreciation, both in business and in government, of the implications of foreign ventures by American business. Their success or failure can indeed affect the lives of literally hundreds of millions of people.

Of the many excellent addresses given at the Fiftieth Anniversary Conference of the Harvard Business School in September 1958, probably the most stirring was that by Charles H. Malik, then Foreign Minister of Lebanon. On February 18, 1959, speaking in Chicago in his role as President of the General Assembly of the United Nations, Malik made some further remarks on the subject of economic development. Although many United States businessmen would not agree fully with his words, they do provide, in my opinion, a forceful epilogue for this chapter. Said Malik:

[Among the special conditions which the economic world faces today are] the rise of the underdeveloped peoples of Asia, Africa, and Latin America who can no longer passively acquiesce to their external exploitation, and who therefore vigorously demand an equitable share in any economic association they may enter into with the more highly developed countries; [and] a general breakdown in morals and standards whereby people think that cleverness and force determine human existence, and whatever you do, provided you can manage to get away with it, is all right; . . .

. . . the Asians and Africans want either to industrialize themselves and thereby become economically independent of the West or, insofar as considerable economic interdependence must persist between them and the more highly developed countries for a long time to come, to have an equitable if not an equal share in the management of enterprises bearing upon their economies. The age of crude exploitation is completely gone, and there is open before all of us today the prospect either of estrangement or of honest cooperation on the basis of equality and mutual respect.

Concerning the underdeveloped countries . . . a wonderful prospect is opening up, namely, partnership. There is no reason to suppose that corporation laws and regulations are sacrosanct, and in our dealings with Asia, Africa, and Latin America, the great Western concerns must henceforth modify their rigidity in favor of much greater flexibility and openness of mind. The concept of nationalization must be viewed as a norm, and whole new systems of partnership between governments and corporations must be sought. The underdeveloped cannot develop themselves without the agency of the developed, and the developed cannot creatively perform this function without the willing consent of the underdeveloped. In this mutuality of need and complementarity of function, we have a natural given condition for the development of better human relations. Let people be guided, therefore, by their higher interests, their higher selves; let them see that the association of equals is far more glorious and stable than the association of superior and native; and let them rise to the joyous level of our common humanity beyond all distinctions of race, color, and even culture. In short, let them be men, and not mere economic exploiters, and the envy, distrust, and recalcitrance of the underdeveloped, as well as the overweening paternalism of the developed, will be overcome.[3]

In his speech at the Fiftieth Anniversary Conference, Malik made another comment which seems particularly apropos to this matter of business responsibility overseas. He referred to the distinction between "imperialists" and the people and companies who make the kind of long-term commitment mentioned by Mr. Blough as an important characteristic of the Merck venture in India. It is the alien, the exploiter, Malik said, who is the object of distrust and fear, not the man who ties his future to that of the other country and takes part with you in the good and the bad that befalls it.

American business is woven into the fabric of our society. It is not an exploiter, but a full-fledged member, gaining and growing as the nation expands, and suffering when it slides backward. If an American business overseas is to fulfill its responsibilities to the nation as an effective participant in the conflict with communism, and to itself as a continuing profit-making enterprise, it would do well to keep this role uppermost in mind.

[3] "Human Relations and the Industrial Order," address delivered before the Midwinter Personnel Conference of the American Management Association, Chicago, February 18, 1959.

RESPONSIBILITIES OF BUSINESS LEADERS—1960

Arthur B. Van Buskirk

AS CITIZENS of the United States, looking at the health of our mid-twentieth-century democracy, we cannot help asking ourselves whether we are in danger of losing the liberties won by our forefathers. Disturbing trends suggest that the changing ideals of our people and the radically altered character of our society may have made obsolescent a governmental system designed nearly 200 years ago. If there be

Note: Mr. Van Buskirk is Vice President and Governor of T. Mellon and Sons, Pittsburgh, and Chairman of the Board of the Federal Reserve Bank of Cleveland.

validity in this possibility, certainly no group of American citizens has a higher degree of responsibility to recognize and to act upon it than our business leaders.

We cannot shrug off this matter casually. Over the long span of history, kings and tyrants have ruled the world; prior to the American Revolution, democracy flourished for only a brief century or two in Greece and Rome and then disappeared. While parliamentary government was formalized in England in the late seventeenth century, it was our Declaration of Independence, followed closely by the French Revolution, that gave rise to democracy in its broad and modern sense.

THE COLONIAL IDEALS

What were the aims and ideals of our founding fathers? God-fearing, adventurous men, they were the sons of colonists who had been drawn to this land by the opportunity to live their own lives free from oppression. It is amazing to note that in a single generation just before the Revolution, after the American wilderness had been settled for more than a century, three colonies with a population of only 1.1 million—Massachusetts, Pennsylvania, and Virginia —produced such great figures as Benjamin Franklin, George Washington, Thomas Jefferson, John Adams, Samuel Adams, James Madison, and John Hancock. These men, like the other colonial leaders, were lovers of freedom and students of political philosophy. They were dedicated to the concept that the people are the source of all authority and that they have the right to change their government whenever it becomes destructive of their happiness. Recognizing this, the founding fathers viewed the federal Constitution as an instrument calculated to preserve the inalienable rights of man which they had asserted in the Declaration of Independence; but they considered the *form of government* they devised as a great experiment which future generations should remold to meet changing times and conditions.

One of the great motivating ideals of colonial days was the belief that every man is required to serve his country in exchange for the liberties which he enjoys. Said Dr. Benjamin Rush, noted Philadelphia physician and signer of the Declaration of Independence, "Every man is public property. His time and talent—his youth—his manhood—his old age—nay more, his life, his all, belong to his country." This same spirit was reflected by young Nathan Hale who, standing near the future site of the United Nations' building, uttered his memorable last words as he faced the hangman's noose.

Thus the entire flower of colonial leadership, the landed gentry like Washington and Jefferson, the merchants, lawyers, doctors, preachers, farmers—old and young alike—served in the colonial governments, the Continental Congresses, and the Constitutional Convention. To each of these early settlers his liberties were his dearest possession; he sought freedom of opinion, freedom of occupation to rise in his chosen calling, and freedom from arbitrary government that would subvert the natural rights of free men.

While the founding fathers trusted the judgment of the majority, they were inherently suspicious of political power. Hence they reserved to the states and the people all power not delegated to the federal government, and they set up the checks and balances with which we are familiar to protect the individual against hasty or ill-considered action of the majority.

A New Society

But they were living in 1776. Contrast our country and society of today with that of two centuries ago. Our nation now spreads from the Atlantic to the mid-Pacific, and our population of 175 million is expected to reach 260 million by 1980. Our basic mode of life is no longer rooted in the soil but in a complex industrial economy founded upon the new technology and geared to the atom, the automobile, the airplane, electricity, and millions of tools, machines, and gadgets. The self-sufficient small community of colonial days has given way to urban life, much of it in great metropolitan centers which are dependent on the functioning of industrialized society as a whole. While only some 5% of the population was living in what might be called an urban environment in 1760 (the combined population of Boston, New York, and Philadelphia was about 150,000), now two thirds of our people live in such areas.

True, when measured by her material wealth, the America of our generation has far surpassed the dreams of her founders—fighting and winning two world wars, overcoming a great depression, and at the same time substantially raising the standard of living of her people. Our nation stands today as the greatest power the world has ever known in terms of industrial might, defense establishment, productive resources, and scientific research. Why, then, should we fear for the outlook of our system of democratic government?

In answer to this question let me first quote from a prophetic observation made by James Bryce, one of the great students of American democracy, writing in 1914. He spoke first of a "part of the Atlantic where the westward-speeding steam vessel always expects to encounter fogs. On the fourth or fifth day of the voyage while still in bright sunlight, one sees at a distance a long, low, dark gray line across the bows, and is told that this is the first of the fog banks" shrouding icebergs with all of their perilous implications. Bryce went on to say:

> So America in her swift onward progress, sees, looming on the horizon and now no longer distant, a time of mists and shadows, wherein dangers lie concealed whose form and magnitude she can scarcely yet conjecture. As she fills up her Western regions with inhabitants, she sees the time approach when all of the best land ... will have been occupied; ... the struggle for existence will become more severe. And while the outlet which the West now provides for the overflow of the great cities will have become less available, the cities will

have grown immensely more populous; ... the chronic evils
and problems of old societies and crowded countries, such as
we see them today in Europe, will have reappeared on this
new soil, while the demand of the multitude to have a larger
share of the nation's collective wealth may well have grown
more insistent.

High economic authorities pronounce that the beginnings
of this time of pressure lie only a few years ahead ... it may
be the time of trial for democratic institutions.[1]

PERIOD OF TRIAL

There seems little doubt that our nation is now passing
through the period of trial predicted by Bryce and that the
fog enshrouds us and the icebergs lie all around us. What
are some of the principal threats to our good ship of state?

First I might mention again the changed character of our
society: a few million colonists rooted in the soil and attracted to public life have been replaced today by vast numbers living in a complex industrialized nation. Masses of our
citizens, feeling they are merely cogs in a machine, share a
group psychology which measures a man's fitness for public
office by his prejudice in favor of the group and his ability
as a radio or television performer—not by his character
and talents.

Jefferson had serious doubts whether democracy would

[1] James Bryce, *The American Commonwealth* (New York, The
Macmillan Company, 1927), II, 912–913.

succeed in a largely urban and industrial nation, and he may well have been right. Democracy may be a species of social luxury unsuited to our present society because we have lost the environment and conditions essential to its operation. Remember that nations and civilizations have come and gone in the course of the world's history. Indeed, in the last two decades we have seen the fall of many important states and the rise of more than 20 new nations. There is no magic in any form of government, nor any assurance that the America we know will survive.

Now it is the essence of democracy that the citizen should give close and unbiased attention to public affairs, recognizing this as his public duty. So it was in ancient Greece and in our colonial days, and so it should be today. Pericles said, "We are a free democracy. We do not allow absorption in our own affairs to interfere with participation in those of Athens."

In contrast, at the very time when American democracy needs in public life the most competent of its citizens, who might be able to deal effectively with complex governmental problems, most of our best leadership either shuns or cannot be elected to public office. This leadership is to be found primarily in the higher ranks of business, in the professions, and in the universities. Here the able and enterprising have been attracted by the financial rewards of industry, or by the freedoms inherent in academic pursuits, or by the desire for a sense of personal achievement in having risen, according to American tradition, to the top ranks in our free enterprise system. This is all fine. It is the essence of the American spirit of liberty. But where does it leave our democracy and our government?

A second "iceberg" threatening our democracy is the growing organization of mass pressure groups using their great political power to induce the government to grant them special privileges. Instead of individual citizens cooperating and competing within the framework of the state, we see vast groups of our fellows, organized and unorganized, embracing the concept of the welfare state, and viewing the federal treasury as a source of individual and collective support in the form of loans, doles, and subsidies. Over 21% of the 1960 federal budget—items totaling $16.7 billion—represents subsidies in one form or another. True, some of these subsidies are necessary or wise because they help the indigent or contribute to economic growth and stability, but a large proportion does not fall into these categories. Washington himself warned in his Farewell Address that powerful factions seeking to serve their selfish interests could in the end destroy public liberty.

A third threat, like ocean currents bearing other ominous icebergs, is a series of trends that are contrary to the morals and ideals of our nation's founders. For at least some of these, you and I must share a measure of responsibility. For instance:

• Extravagant waste of our natural resources and pollution of the air and water around us.

- The corrupting influence of prosperity, which leads to a sordid scramble for power and material riches in the ranks of both management and labor.
- The search for security instead of opportunity and the accompanying erosion of the drive to achieve.
- The unwillingness of the Congress to control the monopolistic power of our labor unions and to adopt stern measures to deal with the shocking corruption in a number of them.
- The coddling of juvenile delinquents.
- Our lack of imagination in meeting the unemployment problem by means other than the dole.
- The apathy in important places toward unbalanced budgets and dangerous inflation.
- Our failure to recognize that the leaders of our thought and culture—teachers and clergymen—must be compensated at a level which will permit them to enjoy a decent standard of living if we are to expect them to support our system.
- The failure to teach our children that government service is a high calling, that hard work offers real satisfaction, and that easy courses in college, campus football stars, and beauty queens are false gods.
- The failure of 40% of our qualified voters to exercise their franchise in national elections.
- The failure of many of our older cities to recognize the serious implications of slums and blighted residential districts—the breeding places for the forces of crime and corruption.
- And, finally, our complacency as over the years we see

an unwarranted extension of the tentacles of the federal bureaucracy into every nook and cranny of our daily lives, and the surrender by the states and the people of the powers intended to be reserved for them by the founders of the republic.

Against the chilly blasts from such icebergs neither a Democratic mink nor a Republican vicuña coat will afford protection.

As to the question of how we are to steer our course and avoid these and other icebergs that threaten to wreck our ship of state, I have a few suggestions which, if inadequate, may at least provoke some thought.

STEERING A SAFE COURSE

First, we should aim for the development of leadership at all levels of government. Our best-qualified men and women from all walks of life must, as in colonial days, be ever ready to heed the call to public service, both in and out of government. Part of the problem is that a free society requires more leaders than do other forms of society. With us the heads of state *lead;* they do not rule. Hence, in each new generation we must develop statesmen, men of broad vision with an understanding of our nation's traditions and a sense of her destiny. The fates have called upon America to lead the West during one of history's most crucial epochs. Two philosophies, each backed by a dynamic economy, struggle for supremacy as the atomic age advances and the space age dawns. Colonialism is disappearing as new and impoverished peoples and nations rise to seek their share of the necessaries of life.

In such a time it is not enough that our leaders have a grasp of our domestic social, political, and economic problems. Many of them must be students of international affairs, schooled in the languages, cultures, and aspirations of other nations, and hence able to guide our policies in world trade wisely and to represent us in the formulation and administration of an enlightened foreign policy. Such leadership, sensitive to the responsibilities that rest upon a nation so richly blessed, could go far to preserve our way of life and to bring a just and lasting peace in the Golden Age that may lie ahead.

True, there is precedent for the hope that in such an age as this the times themselves will produce the kind of talent we need. Democracy has a way of renewing itself and bringing leadership from the ranks of unknown men, seemingly out of the very roots in the soil. Who would have expected the rise of a Lincoln in the days before the Civil War? But often before in history democratic nations have yearned for a Lincoln; yet such a man did not emerge. One reason may lie in the fact that the youth of these nations were not—and are not—given the proper models to look up to. It was when Thomas Jefferson, at the age of 22, heard the stirring words of Patrick Henry that he resolved to dedicate himself to the cause of freedom and independence. Perhaps in your community, company, or home there are young men and women in whom you can kindle the spark that will make them great leaders. If we fail to develop the kind of leadership I have mentioned, it is entirely possible that the self-serving, unscrupulous Hoffas will eventually establish a welfare state and assume dictatorial power over our formerly free society.

In addition to enlightened leaders spending full time in public service, we must develop new techniques by which our best citizens may voluntarily enlist to aid public officials in the solution of our civic problems at the municipal and state level. Perhaps the greatest significance of Pittsburgh's renaissance since the last war lies in the unique association of government officials and top business leaders forged into a single team, irrespective of political affiliation, that carried the program through.

My second suggestion for avoiding the "icebergs" is the reawakening of our citizenry to the traditions and ideals that have made our nation strong: the power of religion in men's souls and of freedom in their spirits; the knowledge that for the individual as well as the nation the road to the heights is built by hard work and sacrifice. All our citizens must know that the price of freedom is service, that the unity of the states and of the people will always be the keystone of our strength as a nation, and that in a democracy we must each strive to overcome the differences that divide us and to strengthen the bonds that unite us as free Americans. Tolerance is part of the essence of democracy. Jefferson gave the bust of Madison, his arch opponent, a place of honor just inside the entrance door at Monticello.

You may ask: "Who is to do this reawakening?" Quite

obviously it should begin in the home, and it must be continued in our churches, schools, and universities. Here in their formative years our youth must receive from inspired parents, clergymen, and teachers the vision of our country's greatness and identify themselves with it. Alfred North Whitehead has put it thus: "Moral education is impossible apart from the habitual vision of greatness.... We are at the threshold of a democratic age, and it remains to be determined whether the equality of man is to be realized on a high level or a low level. There was never a time in which it was more essential to hold before young people the vision of greatness." [2] Our whole system of education, including adult education, should adopt as one of its primary aims the training of citizens for their public duties and the development of a widespread understanding of the conditions which make democracy succeed or fail.

This spiritual reawakening must also come from our business leaders. The voices of the managers of free enterprise must constantly be heard throughout the land telling the meaning of our competitive profit system, with its inherent opportunities and responsibilities, and dramatizing our American heritage. And we must willingly help to remold the structure of free enterprise to match its greater size, its greater goals, and its greater concern with human beings. We must not tolerate business practices or ethics which will make of our corporations anything less than fair-minded,

[2] *The Aims of Education and Other Essays* (New York, The Macmillan Company, 1929), pp. 106–107.

respected employers, good citizens in their communities, and watchful servants of the public welfare.

A third major step in avoiding the "icebergs" and adapting our democratic government to present times must come from broad and basic research in the art of self-government. How extraordinary that with all of our emphasis on science, and on pure and applied research in almost every field, we have thus far failed to establish a national laboratory in political science!

My suggestion is that there should be created—perhaps under the sponsorship of the National Academy of Sciences or of a group of our great universities—a meeting ground where the ablest statesmen of both parties and scholars in the arts and techniques of self-government could meet together periodically and study the workings of our democracy. They should be free to make the boldest kind of recommendations: for example, that we should adopt the British system with a president, a prime minister, and parliamentary responsibility. Other fertile fields for their study in the light of changed conditions could be: a re-examination of the delegation of powers to the federal government and the domain in which state action should be final; the antiquated method of electing the President and Vice President through the electoral college; the administration of the presidency with its killing burdens; an expanded role of responsibility for the vice presidency; the composition of the cabinet; the development of methods by which our political parties can be financed so that elected officials will not feel beholden to their major financial supporters.

Similarly, such a group of political scientists might make recommendations at the state level on the reconstitution and unification of government in metropolitan areas, so that our older cities might adequately cope with problems arising from suburban expansion and the deterioration of their central business districts. Perhaps I should add that, in my opinion, the Hoover Commission did a fine job in studying how to make our government operations more efficient, and this too we must continue. But I am thinking of something more basic that goes to the heart of our governmental system and recognizes that the founding fathers realized that their handiwork was a great experiment and expected us to remold it to meet changing times. To this task each succeeding generation should devote its best creative energies. Studies of these matters by committees of the Congress are normally unsatisfactory because of the political considerations that influence their findings.

Fortunately, the span of our lives is lengthening in this age of medical research, and with the approach of the sundown most of us, before it is night, are still assured of a long, quiet evening to devote to worthwhile matters. Will Durant tells us that in every age and nation civilization is the product, privilege, and responsibility of the minority who find the leisure and energy to think their own thoughts unswayed by the attitudes of the majority. And as the shadows fall, relative values clarify. Power and money and titles no longer sway the judgment. We discover that much of our time as managers of business has been spent on the merry-go-round grabbing for brass rings. Fortunate is the man who learns in younger years, with Thomas Jefferson, that there may be even loftier goals than high office. When Jefferson came to write his epitaph, he never mentioned having been President of the United States. He wished to be remembered as the founder of the University of Virginia and author of the Declaration of Independence.

In conclusion, then, today democracy issues her imperatives to all inheritors of the American birthright—but especially to you and me as business and civic leaders. The foghorns are blowing. From the bridge comes the call, "Icebergs ahead!" On freedom's ship we can each, if we will, take a turn at the wheel—or we can go on grabbing for brass rings. Which it shall be for any one of us only the voice of his conscience can answer. Mencken said in jest that a conscience is "that inner something that tells us somebody's looking." But in all seriousness I say to you: "Somebody is looking. It is our children, our children's children, and the generations of Americans yet unborn."

BUSINESSMEN WHO
THINK GREATLY

Adlai E. Stevenson

ALFRED NORTH WHITEHEAD once said: "A great society is a society in which its men of business think greatly of their function." Are American businessmen today "thinking greatly"? I say no; and thus I am cast in the role of critic, setting out to state bluntly what seem to me to be the obligations, especially the unmet obligations, of the business community to the community at large.

I appreciate fully my danger. A request for criticism is

Note: Mr. Stevenson is the former Governor of Illinois and the Democratic candidate for the Presidency in 1952 and 1956.

not always to be taken at face value, and the critic is not always popular as I have some reason to know. But I am not unaccustomed to the task.

I have been a businessman's lawyer most of my life and have had some trouble "thinking greatly" myself, let alone telling my friends and clients how to think greatly about the future of society. But surely there is serious unease in the nation and the world, and it is time for *some* thinking, difficult as it may be. None of us is satisfied with the way things are going; we are surrounded by both troubles and opportunities.

And the businessman, although he has lost much of his former influence, is still "central" in and indispensable to the American and world system. So it is imperative that he, of all people, "think greatly," that he assume a more objective and influential role in the larger concerns of the new equalitarian society that is emerging here and everywhere in this age of revolution.

I think of the prayer of a little English boy in World War II: "God bless Mother and Daddy, my brother and sister, and save the King! And, oh God, do take care of yourself, because if anything happens to you we're all sunk!" Please don't think that I am equating business and God. I'm a Democrat and you have not fooled me! But the pivotal position of business and the business manager in our society must be obvious to any serious student of our system.

How have businessmen done so far in these respects? My answer is "not well enough." The great changes that have taken place in America in the past 50 years have been effected most of the time over the protest of the business community. Business fought bitterly, for instance, against increasing graduation of the income tax; against the Social Security program and the minimum-wage law; against unemployment compensation and the strengthening of collective bargaining; against enlarged housing and educational programs; against TVA and other natural resource developments; against farm price protection; against foreign aid.

The plain fact is—without arguing the "rightness" or "wrongness" of any one of these policies—that in the judgment of the community, American business has been wrong, shortsighted, and more interested in profit than people, in dollars than ends. Two hundred years ago Rousseau said: "As soon as public service ceases to be the chief business of the citizens and they would rather serve with their money than their persons, the State is not far from its fall."

It is not easy to find an explanation for this record of failure. I think the business community is the victim of an intellectual time-lag. In the span of about 50 years we have altered the whole physical apparatus of our lives. We have conquered space, split the atom, lengthened life, doubled the world's population, and launched the interplanetary adventure. Yet, although everything is changed, we all sense that our thinking about the aims, scope, and performance of our economic system has not kept pace; that at least in some degree stereotypes, ideology, prejudice, even myths, have taken the place of that re-examination and self-analysis from which no human society ought to be long divorced. To a considerable extent, the businessman is both the victim and the perpetrator of this unhealthy situation.

Enough of the obvious. The important fact now is that in these times of violent change the nation desperately needs to have the American business community reoriented and assured of itself and its direction once again. We face great thickets of tangled dilemmas which cannot be solved without great thinking and mighty actions in which the business community must play a leading role. Taken together—and I hope I do not sound melodramatic—these problems are placing the American system on trial for its life.

Many of the issues pose direct challenges to our economic system, for which the businessman is primarily responsible; all of them have economic overtones. So a realistic re-examination of our economic system and its state of readiness is a responsibility business and industry cannot, must not, evade or postpone.

Let me suggest a few of the major questions in the economic sphere which are lodged firmly in the laps of American business managers, and which demand a new look at our economic machine.

(1) The most important is the disparity in living standards over the world—measured roughly by average income of $2,000 per year in North America as against $100 or less for more than half of the world's population. And the rich are getting richer and the poor poorer all the time.

(2) The communist worldwide economic offensive, which gives us cause for greater concern than does communist military strength. To maintain the balance of power, if for no other reason, the West will have to make a greater effort to provide an alternative to communism as a technique of change and growth in the vast underdeveloped areas. Brains and sensitivity are as important as money.

(3) The huge social-capital requirements at home for education, housing, health, urban renewal, resource development, and the like.

(4) The control of inflation without depression.

I could go on; but I hope this brief list of our larger concerns suggests that the priorities, values, philosophy, and emphases in our society must be adjusted to some tough realities. Our traditional standards and goals—an ever higher standard of living here at home and an ever more comfortable life for ourselves—will not do for this age. If we persist in them, they will prove inadequate to the times. And the road of history is marked by the whitened bones of civilizations which were based on a set of goals that the passage of time had made obsolete.

Can it be done in peace time? Can a society wrench itself free from a set of values that have become a strait-jacket and reclothe itself in more suitable fashions? Even under the threat of a powerful opponent and of mankind's self-annihilation, can people perform this mighty action, and the great thinking which must underlie it? Frankly, I do not know. But I do know that to see that we do is the very top responsibility of business—yes, and labor, and all the rest of us, too.

One of the parts of our new garment of values must be sustained, substantial economic growth. To achieve the level of growth we need, we may have to make some sacrifices in taxes and prejudices. We may have to turn from the temptations of more leisure and less work, of simple routine and standardization, to irritating, demanding innovation instead. But it is clear that we cannot meet the relentless foreign and domestic challenges without sustained economic growth.

Superficially, our concern with economic advance arises from the loud words of Mr. Khrushchev, who is voicing the changed direction of the Marxist attack. Since the communists can no longer aim their barbs at poverty and misery in our system, they must find some other target. Curiously enough for a revolutionary, antibourgeois movement, they are now saying that our way cannot produce as high a living standard as rapidly as their's can. By the very nature of a free enterprise economy, they tell us, we cannot grow steadily or hope to keep pace with communism's surging advance of 7% or 8% a year. "We will bury you," says Mr. Khrushchev, "not under hydrogen missiles but under a flood of production which will finally prove to the Russian people and to the world at large that 'we can do everything you can do better,' and do a lot of things in addition which you cannot do at all." And to prove his point, Khrushchev is driving the Soviet Union to catch up with America, and has proclaimed this as his main domestic aim.

Here then is the new challenge—the challenge represented by the competition of sustained growth secured by government direction. The communist performance since the war —both in Russia and China—is formidable enough for us to take the challenge seriously. We can no longer take our own productive, scientific, and technological superiority for granted.

But this gauntlet is not the real—or, at least, the only— reason that we must devote ourselves to economic growth. We have demonstrable human needs unsatisfied at home and heavy obligations overseas. Consequently, the communists' challenge—that they and only they know how to grow rapidly and indefinitely—becomes relevant not only in itself but also in terms of the great contest of the future. We must grow for our own sake because of three facts:

- The first is our rapidly expanding birth rate. We are growing by about 2% every year, an increase as large as India's. This wave first hits our homes and cities, then our schools, and at last our labor force where, when combined with a 3% increase in productivity, it will call for more jobs at a rate approaching 5% a year.

- Secondly, we have a long backlog of undone tasks left by the depression, then the World War, and then the Korean War—old schools, old hospitals, old houses, blighted city areas, rural slums, limited water supply, air pollution.

Each year increases the backlog. Estimates put our needs
for public services of all kinds at a figure as high as $9
billion. Possibly it is more.

- Finally, we are faced with the aggressive pressure of Russia. The largest single load our economy bears is the defense budget. Nor is the Soviet challenge only military.
Their program of trade and aid to underdeveloped areas
will increase as Soviet growth (and, let us hope, disarma-
ment) releases more resources for their campaign to win
the uncommitted and strategic areas. Our basic research,
too, must be accelerated, if we are not to see Russian military teams winking at us from every planet.

Russian advances in production and increased economic
assistance are bound to increase the attraction of the communist system in the decisive underdeveloped areas. And
this may do something else: having assumed our superiority for so long, for the Russians to overtake us in the
economic sphere will be a greater shock to the American
people than Sputnik and Lunik, and leave us confused, un-
certain, and even more vulnerable to half-truths and false
prophets—just when what we need to hear above the old
cacophony of politics and business is the clear, clean, astrin-
gent note of the trumpet.

In one sense America has less difficulty in answering this
challenge—which, it seems to me, requires an annual growth
rate of 3% to 4%—than any other nation on earth or in history. In terms of the physical components of growth—materials, manpower, installed capacity, managerial capacity, and

technical skills—we have all of them in vast amounts and any we do not have we can import. We have already seen— in such crises as the Korean War—that production can be greatly expanded in our economy, once we decide to do it. The task of achieving a smaller but steadier expansion is certainly not beyond our powers.

Perhaps the answer lies in administrative mechanics. Maybe, for instance, the task of plotting the economy's broad course needs some strengthening of the President's economic advisers or the substitution of a national economic advisory council with members drawn from the main interests in the economy. It could be so. But for my part I think the key lies buried far deeper than this; I suspect we will find it in that system of values which I mentioned earlier, and I further suspect that it is the lack of will, not way, which is keeping us from attaining the growth we need right now.

How do you go about acquiring a new set of values? I must confess that I am not sure. But I am certain that the first step is the stripping away of outworn prejudices and misfitting notions which prevent us from seeing the need for something new. So while we are "thinking greatly," I am going to do a little hoping greatly—that in the future the attitudes of business will not be entirely determined by pre-existing prejudice and incendiary rhetoric about the American way of life, while the Soviet way of life creeps across the earth. Is it too much to ask business to help us graduate from the nineteenth century, to throw off the semantic shackles of the dear, dead past, and get into position to meet the full scale of the real and rising attack on our way of life?

In this matter of achieving economic growth, I can see at least three battered and shopworn articles of clothing which the American businessman is still insisting on wearing: his notions on inflation, on the role of government in the economy, and on the real purposes of his business.

Let us start with inflation. It is obvious that rising prices are a real danger, and policies for dealing with them successfully offer one of the greatest challenges to democratic capitalism. Unhappily, however, the exaggeration, misstatement, and fallacy which have beset the discussion of this issue often make it an exercise not of reason but of ideology.

In the first place, we are *not* on the verge of a runaway inflation as the recent propaganda would have us believe. To suggest that we are shakes people's confidence further and encourages the very inflation against which it is supposed to warn us. Although there had been little price inflation for more than a year by early 1959, government financing was acutely embarrassed and our gold was draining away.

Another common cry is that the value of the dollar has fallen by more than half in the last 50 years. Certainly it has —but over the same period the economy has grown fourfold and the vast majority of Americans have many more dollars to spend. It is growth, startling growth, that has raised our living standards to their present unequalled height. Those who fear inflation to the point of stopping growth might be able to maintain the present living standard. But they would ensure that it grew no further.

Perhaps the most encrusted fallacies cling around the idea that only government spending is inflationary. This bit of nonsense we hear repeated over and over by top officials in industry and government. "We must hold down the federal budget," they wail, "because government spending is inflationary." This theme even bids fair to replace that tired old howl of the pessimists and the "antis": "We are spending ourselves into bankruptcy!"

The fact is that in a state of accelerating demand there is no mystic difference between *public* and *private* expenditure. A government order for a tank or a private order for a tractor have an identical effect on the demand for steel, machine tools, skilled labor, and so forth. Either public or private bidding can cause an inflationary movement. The government sparked growth—and inflation—in 1950 because of the Korean War. Private industry sparked growth—and inflation—in 1955 by expanding investment. Yet the mythical distinction between public and private spending still dominates our minds.

I suppose this is just the latest blossom on the hardy old idea that all public spending is bad and all private spending good. But the crucial question in assessing both the inflationary impact of an expenditure and its "goodness" or "badness" is: "What is the money being spent on?" and not "Who is spending it?" We—and businessmen particularly—need to look at public spending objectively, judging each

item by where it is going and what we are purchasing with
it. In my view, Oliver Wendell Holmes summed it up when
he said: "With my taxes I buy civilization." Education, personal security, a decent urban environment, and, today, survival in a threatened world—are these not more vital than
the hairdos, the cosmetics, the drinks and tranquilizers, the
chromium-encrusted cars and amusements which belong to
the area of private spending?

In America more is spent per head on advertising than on
education. A starlet can earn in a month five years' salary of
a school teacher. Shining new cars stand beside gutters often
choked with the refuse of a careless, wasteful people. Mul-
tiply your own instances. In fact, as Professor Galbraith has
reminded us, the private sector is so well stocked that we
have to go to unparalleled lengths of persuasion to keep
goods moving and persuade the public to develop wants
they never knew they had.

It seems a little ludicrous to hand over such vital human
needs as security, education, and a wide range of welfare services to the public purse because they are so vital, and then
proceed to starve them simply because they are public. I am
not saying, of course, that all government spending is good.
What I am saying is that most of it is good, and that you
will not find all the extravagance on the public side by any
means.

In other words, inflation is not caused simply by government spending or simply by private spending. Before the
First World War, when there were no large taxes, no large

government spending, no deficits, no debt, and no unions to speak of, the average increase in inflationary pressure was just over 2% a year. This average is higher than in the last decade if you exclude 1950 and 1955. But then, if you exclude those years, you also get very little growth. We have achieved fairly stable prices recently—incidentally, simultaneous with a $13 billion government deficit—but at the cost of stagnancy. If private production falls off by over 20%, government obviously can spend a lot before all the slack is taken up and pressure begins to mount again.

So the conservatives offer us sound money, but do not add that we may have to be content with, say, a 1% rate of growth. The liberals offer us a 5% rate of growth, but discount the risk of a 2% to 3% annual inflation.

As for the business community, the weight of its influence has been on the side of security and stability rather than enterprise, opportunity, and growth. It has rarely even tried to find an answer to the stubborn problem of how to achieve adequate growth *and* stability. So far, its only suggestion has been slacks and recessions to "shake out prices." But in this last recession, some prices, particularly in industries of highly organized labor and imperfect competition, continued to go up. Nor do slack times do very much to make good the backlog of public needs. Above all, by recessions we export the instability of capitalism for all to see. Rhodesia and the Congo have had to endure close to a 50% fall in copper prices; the primary material areas have all suffered comparable and unsettling price losses which

quickly cancel out our economic aid. In short, the remedy
of recurrent recession is no remedy and brings on other
maladies just as grave.

We could, I believe, restrain the pressure on prices gen-
erated by the full use of our resources if we were ready to
exercise some self-restraint on wage and price increases.
Other democratic communities have done it. In Holland and
Sweden, the trade union movement agreed on at least two
occasions to accept lower wages at a time of international
pressure on the country's balance of payments. Germany's
price stability during the period of rapid growth after 1948
was due in part to the restraint shown by German labor. Are
voluntary wage freezes and price reductions, especially in
times of high profits, beyond our economic statesmanship in
the inflation struggle? And certainly long, crippling strikes
in basic industries are a severe indictment when we are in
competition with the most powerful and disciplined opponent in our history.

If restraint is not forthcoming from the parties involved,
what then? Are we helpless—with so much at stake? If
you businessmen do not come up with some better answer
than recurrent recession you will grievously embarrass capitalism, and "the public" will produce a solution—acting
through government. And that answer will be more government, not less.

Another ideological blinder which limits our vision and
sharply reduces our ability to make sound, objective decisions

is the old, familiar refrain that any government supervision spells "socialism" and the ruin of free enterprise.

Socialism is the public ownership of the means of production, and no one is proposing that. But as we use the word, it seems to be any government authority we do not like. Of course, things we like—tariffs, subsidies, mail concessions, support prices, tax write-offs, depletion allowances, and government aids to particular groups—are rarely denounced as "socialism," except perhaps by the group's competitors.

A farsighted government policy, designed to strengthen our country, improve our education, rebuild our cities, extend our services, and ensure a steady growth in our productive capacity, far from being the enemy of private enterprise, is the precondition of capitalism's successful competition with communism. It is the ally of free enterprise because it creates and maintains the climate within which individual initiative can flourish. Consciously designed to release individual enterprise and provide a well-nourished garden within which it can flower, public action can be private enterprise's greatest benefactor. I will go further and say that government is the indispensable ally of individual enterprise.

Actually only once has private enterprise been in danger of extinction in America. That was in 1929 when, without taxes, big government, big deficits, or big unions, it all but killed itself. Its prestige was vastly increased by the bursting growth of the Second World War. And after the government-sparked expansion resulting from Korea, we got not socialism but four or five of the best years private enterprise has ever had—and even a Republican administration! Similarly, European enterprise was rescued from the stagnation of the Twenties and Thirties by a plan launched at Harvard by a great American, George C. Marshall. As a result, socialism has receded in Europe, and public ownership is being abandoned even by socialists.

Intelligent government action is not, I repeat, the enemy but the essential complement of effective private enterprise, and it is all the more imperative when we are confronted by the central planning of the Soviet Union. If government's functions are growing, so are the complexities of our life, the crowding up of our country, and our involvement in the world. A Jeffersonian dream that "the best government is the least government" belongs to a century when America was isolated and empty. Today it could leave us defenseless before a challenge neither Jefferson nor any of the founding fathers could have possibly foreseen.

In the business world, it is not the rise of big government that gives you problems you never had or never faced up to before. In reality what you face is the forces that bring big government about. This is a big world. We have big enemies. The interests in our own country—of management and labor —are big, too, and could well become "overmighty subjects" and restore the confusion and enmity of the old feudal monopolies. In all this, government big enough to meet its responsibilities is a condition of survival. We live, day in, day out, with the great challenges of the world at large and with the great perplexities at home of a vastly increasing population. We must not be afraid of and we cannot get along without government built to their scale.

I do not ask you to agree with all I have been saying. I realize that one man's cliché can be another man's conviction. And surely there will always be sharp disagreement about the relation of government and citizens, corporate or individual. But I am deeply concerned by what I interpret as a fixation in the business community, that government is a "bad thing." Like any fixation, this one is risky at any time. In this moment, it is dangerous. Look back through history and you will find that the most penetrating and subversive attacks always come up, as it were, on the blind side, in the area where rigidity and complacency and prejudice have taken the place of thought and questioning and adaptability. Under the Manchus, no Confucian gentleman would concern himself with the scientific nonsense of the alchemists. The formidable increase in Western power based on science and technology was disregarded because science was held in such low repute. Significantly, today it is precisely by the bold use of government that the communists challenge us most gravely—spending more proportionately on arms, aid, education, and research because government can so allot the nation's resources. We shall not change this challenge simply by rejecting the instruments our foes are using. Many of us dislike the thought of government as passionately and irrationally as the Confucians rejected science. Perhaps this is the very reason why we should be ready to give it a long, new look.

Finally, a word about the purposes of a business enterprise. In the past, businessmen have driven rails across a vast continent, tamed a wilderness, released a flood of goods and services by paying primary attention to their own self-interest. That personal concern, intertwined as it was with the success of the companies they set up to gratify it, did the job of the day—though not without exacting its price.

But the rule in today's world is that man's larger interest is everywhere breaking in upon his immediate short-term interest and overriding it. This applies to business, just as to the other concerns of people. This is the logic of a unifying, contracting world, where time and distance become daily shorter; and if we deplore it, we still cannot turn the tide back. Because you are now more than ever dependent on your environment, one in which "rugged individualism" is an illusion, you will increasingly have to resolve your conflicts on the basis of what is best for that environment. Or, to put it bluntly, what is best for society. Like it or not, the business of the modern corporation is society. And smaller businesses, which are less obviously concerned with the whole life of their stockholders and suppliers, workers, and customers, will increasingly find that their business, too, is society.

I do not need to say here how much that society needs the

BUSINESSMEN WHO THINK GREATLY 157

talents of the businessman. He has a gift for realism. His ideas are constantly tested by action, and he never gets far away from the practical. His motive is fundamentally optimistic. He has a rare capacity to resist adversity, and to keep coming back to the job until it is somehow done. He has drive and courage, when they are aroused and the incentive is good.

It is the incentive that counts, of course. Ours is an incentive system, which is the businessman's way of saying this is a system of individual men and women who are not compelled but who choose to do what they wish to do. But there are many kinds of incentive. Your incentive, after all, is what you decide it will be. It can be profit. It can be power. It can also be the satisfaction of making a humane mark on your time, of building a better life for the people and the community around you. These are incentives, too, if you will make them so. They are also values that society desperately needs. And they are values which people in distant places, who have more to do with our destiny than we like to think, hold higher than we always have.

America, for the first time in history, has built a productive system operated for the benefit of all the people, speaking by and large, and not for the privileged few. Considering the tenacity of privilege down through the centuries, and the many areas where it still holds unequal sway, this is an achievement on the heroic scale. The builder of this new type of system was business. But business did not think it all up. The American political system gave it its sense of direction, and there were sometimes terrible strains as the two pulled against each other.

Some may say, given my peculiar background, and because of the relationship between the two systems, that what I mean is that businessmen should get into politics. This topic is, I know, a very lively one in the business community today. As a matter of fact, it could be the latest fad, succeeding "human relations" and "management development." To some extent, I *am* saying this. You bear a heavy responsibility for the Republic's well-being and democracy's survival. The immediate means by which this is achieved—the arena of decision making—is government, and the machinery of choosing the government is politics. The health of both is the first business of every businessman, like every other citizen. But by "getting into politics" I am not recommending that you participate in order to push some particular economic viewpoint or the special interests of your company or industry. What we need, and better have a good deal more of, quickly, is concern for the *national* interest, and not the selfish interest of business, labor, farmers, or any single economic, racial, or religious group.

But what *is* the national interest? All of us, of course, have a slightly different view on that question, as we see readily when the issues of the day are fought out. The difficulty with the business community is that its concept of the public interest is so often limited to individual companies or at most to business as a whole. Consequently, the intellectuals and the politicians, not the businessmen, have taken the lead in shaping national thinking on public affairs. You have, in a sense, abandoned the field. Instead of putting the labor of thought into the job of articulating your views on the shape of American society, your time is spent with your lawyers and your lobbyists and your public relations officers on how to argue "your side" of the case. And you complained because "someone else" was creating a bad public image of American business.

So I am saying "participate in politics," but I am saying, even more, "beware of your heavy responsibility in our system, think through your real objectives, and evolve a vision of the America you would like to see that must take account of considerations above and beyond the success of any business."

Twenty-eight years ago, Alfred North Whitehead stood before an audience here at the Harvard Business School and talked of the role of what he called the business mind. "Mankind is now in one of its rare moods of shifting its outlook," he said. And in this new perspective, "the motive of success is not enough. It produces a short-sighted world which destroys the sources of its own prosperity." Then he came to his point, and the point of this book. "We must not fall into the fallacy," he said, "of thinking of the business world in abstraction from the rest of the community." And he defined the aims of business in this epic phrase: "The general greatness of the community."

That says it.